Pastoral Care and the Means of Grace

Pastoral Care and the Means of Grace

Fortress Press
Minneapolis

RALPH L. UNDERWOOD

for
Alice B. Underwood

PASTORAL CARE AND THE MEANS OF GRACE

Copyright © 1993 Augsburg Fortress. All rights reserved. Except for brief quotations in critical articles or reviews, no part of this book may be reproduced in any manner without prior written permission from the publisher. Write to: Permissions, Augsburg Fortress, 426 S. Fifth St., Box 1209, Minneapolis, MN 55440.

Scripture quotations unless otherwise noted are from the New Revised Standard Version Bible, copyright © 1989 by the Division of Christian Education of the National Council of the Churches of Christ in the United States.

Excerpts are used by permission from the English translation of *Rite of Christian Initiation of Adults,* copyright © 1985 International Committee on English in the Liturgy, Inc. All rights reserved.

Excerpts from *The Church of South India Book of Common Worship* are reprinted by permission of Oxford University Press.

The narrative passage on pages 49-50 is used by permission of the writer, Roberto L. Gómez.

Sections of chapters 1 and 2 are based on "The Presence of God in Pastoral Care Ministry" in *Austin Seminary Bulletin* 101/4 (October 1985), and are used by permission of Austin Presbyterian Theological Seminary.

Cover photo: Sand ripples formed under water, by Ron Church. Reprinted by permission of Photo Researchers, Inc.

Cover and interior design: Spangler Designteam

Library of Congress Cataloging-in-Publication Data

Underwood, Ralph L.
    Pastoral care and the means of grace / Ralph L. Underwood.
        p.   cm.—(Fortress resources for preaching)
    Includes bibliographical references and index.
    ISBN 0-8006-2589-7 (alk. paper)
    1. Pastoral theology.   2. Clergy—Office.   I. Title.   II. Series.
BV4011.U53   1993
253—dc20   92-18311
                                                            CIP

The paper used in this publication meets the minimum requirements of American National Standard for Information Sciences—Permanence of Paper for Printed Library Materials, ANSI Z329.48-1984. ∞™

Manufactured in the U.S.A.   AF 1-2589

97   96   95   94   93   1   2   3   4   5   6   7   8   9   10

Contents

Preface

In this book the means of grace are discussed in relation to pastoral care. The various chapters present prayer as the soul of pastoral care, the presence of God as the thematic bond between pastoral care and the means of grace, reconciliation as the evangelical principle of pastoral care, *divina lectio* (divine reading) as the substance of pastoral care, baptism as the foundation of pastoral care, and the Eucharist as the eschatological horizon of pastoral care. These images disclose the essential interrelation of pastoral care and the means of grace.

No one approaches texts without presuppositions and biases. These prejudices, I believe, heat up the tension that already exists in any text. In doing so, they preclude some avenues for understanding and introduce others. I cannot interpret a liturgical text as a liturgiologist, or even as a participating member of a liturgical church. I bring to such texts my own free church background, my pastoral experience, some psychological knowledge, and a keen interest in the metaphors housed in the text. Although some cases will be presented, they illustrate points and are not subjected to a thoroughgoing reflection for theological construction. This means that the movement of thought tends to proceed from the gathered people of God to the personal lives of individuals in pastoral situations, and not from the personal to the community. These factors inevitably will direct and limit the interpretation.

This book is but an interim report. I hope that it helps readers to reflect constructively on their own ambivalence about the place of the means of grace in their own lives and pastoral ministry. If the intention is realized in any significant measure, then readers will discover new avenues for thought about their ministry, avenues of thought that generate more questions and help to renew hopeful engagement in pastoral ministry.

I am thankful to my colleagues on the faculty of Austin Presbyterian Theological Seminary and to the board of trustees for their generosity in granting me a sabbatical study leave in 1989–90, so that I was able to devote myself to the writing of this book. I am also grateful to Westminster College for accepting me as a Senior Associate during my stay in Cambridge, England, and to Dr. Martin Cressey, Principal of Westminster College, his wife Dr. Pamela Cressey, and the faculty for their gracious hospitality. Editors Timothy Staveteig and Julie Odland of Fortress Press have impressed me with their congenial and practical help on this book. I am grateful.

Introduction: The Renewal of Pastoral Care

For many pastors and counselors, providing pastoral care is like being a member of a fire-fighting crew—long periods of boredom between sudden alarms and exhausting activity. Some days and nights are consumed with running from one emergency to another. Although pastors still give priority to crises, many are devoting fewer hours to other kinds of pastoral visits, sometimes because they find such visits boring, trite, or pointless. In this century the pastoral care movement has issued a clarion call for personal authenticity in ministry. This emphasis on personal effectiveness has contributed, ironically, to a decline in pastoral care ministry except in the forms of crisis ministry and, for a limited number of clergy, psychologically oriented counseling ministry. One result is that ministry with marginalized persons such as elderly shut-ins is neglected in order to accommodate increased pressures toward busyness. Another consequence is that many pastors view much of their ministry as so much social work, a good measure of which is neither rewarding nor necessary.

The current emphasis on personal genuineness, then, has been important for many ordained ministers, but it has not resolved the dilemmas and conflicts that they experience. This is because such "ministries of presence" do not open up to the fullness of the transcendent dimension, without which pastoral ministry is not ministry. What many are seeking today is a new image of pastoral ministry, one that incorporates personal authenticity and presence into the kind of encounter with the holy that is not reducible to psychodynamic analysis.

This book maintains that renewal of pastoral care today depends on a reappropriation of explicitly religious resources—means of grace—in a

1

manner that balances transcendence, freedom, and order. The emphasis on personal presence has highlighted the freedom dimension of what is holy. Yet freedom cannot function without boundaries that give order. Such freedom and order issue from an encounter with what transcends all that we do and are. We lack the transcendent mostly because we lack the ritual dimension in pastoral care.

Renewing attention to religious resources in pastoral ministry has its risks. Often the means of grace have ceased in renewal efforts to function as means and have become the goal, or *religious*—a discrete segment of life esteemed more highly than "secular" life. But God is God, the only end, the author of all life, who cannot be compartmentalized. New attention to religious resources in pastoral ministry, I believe, can strengthen such ministry and open it even more fully to all of life before God. Is it possible to incorporate ritual, with its order and transcendence while at the same time strengthening freedom?

William Clebsch and Charles Jaekle provide us a working definition of pastoral care, which will be revised as the discussion proceeds: "The ministry of the cure of souls, or pastoral care, consists of helping acts, done by *representative Christian persons,* directed toward the *healing, sustaining, guiding, and reconciling* of *troubled persons* whose troubles arise in *the context of ultimate meanings and concerns.*"[1] Although the focus in pastoral care is on ministry with individuals and small groups, pastoral care is embedded in the larger contexts of worship and the church's mission as well as prevailing social, political, and cultural conditions. With the means of grace as a central theme, this book attends directly to both public worship and pastoral care as movements in one pastoral ministry.

Whether one's church tradition is liturgical or free, recovery of the religious dimension of pastoral care entails attention to ritual, which may be formal or informal. Jonathan Z. Smith has noted that the probably false etymology of "religious," from *relegere,* "meaning to gather together, to collect, to go over again, to review mentally, to repeat," nonetheless offers a correct insight that religious thought "requires that this exegetical activity be understood as a constant preoccupation."[2] The question is not whether we include ritual in pastoral care but how doing so can renew ministry, strengthen freedom, and enhance faithfulness in pastoral care.

1. William A. Clebsch and Charles R. Jaekle, *Pastoral Care in Historical Perspective: An Essay with Exhibits* (New York: Harper and Row, 1964), 4.

2. Jonathan Z. Smith, *Imagining Religion: From Babylon to Jonestown* (Chicago: University of Chicago Press, 1982), 38.

Renewal Movements

CLINICAL PASTORAL EDUCATION

This book comes out of my interest in renewal in Christian life and ministry. Renewal is one of God's great gifts. Clinical Pastoral Education (C.P.E.) was a renewing encounter for me, and out of this educational experience I came to realize that the C.P.E. movement has served as a renewal movement in many religious institutions. In its origins, the modern pastoral care movement, centered in C.P.E., was responding to revolutionary developments. William James, Sigmund Freud, and Carl Jung represented the revolution in psychological thinking and practice. This revolution altered the way persons think about themselves and engendered more dynamic forms of self-understanding. Anton Boisen adopted this dynamic turn and the educational method of John Dewey, which was based in the pragmatic philosophy of learning by doing. Boisen molded these into a new image: persons as "living human documents." Boisen also embraced a theological revolution: the social gospel, represented by the Baptist minister Walter Rauschenbusch. This led to an emphasis on ministry with the poor and the marginal, the compromised persons of society. For Boisen himself and for many in the early C.P.E. movement, the mental patient was the one who represented persons facing religious crises, the one to be visited in Christ's name, the one who had much to teach others.

Since those early days the pastoral care and counseling movement has matured and been routinized to a considerable extent. Organizations such as the Association of Clinical Pastoral Education (A.C.P.E.), the National Association of Catholic Chaplains, and the American Association of Pastoral Counselors are large and bureaucratic, and some of their members worry about a loss of vitality, creativity, and even authenticity. Originally on the margins of theological education, C.P.E. now is common among seminary students and others who account for about eight thousand C.P.E. units awarded annually by A.C.P.E.

LITURGICAL RENEWAL

The liturgical renewal movement is a second significant source of change and renewal for pastoral care and counseling. Committed to vitality and renewal of faith and life before God, this movement is a source of renewal beyond the borders of the liturgical denominations and their pastors. This is so because a much larger number of persons from liturgical traditions are active and exercise creative leadership in today's pastoral care organizations than was the case with earlier generations when white, male, Protestant liberals dominated the field. Working in ecumenical settings and participating in ecumenical organizations, these individuals are having an impact on a wide variety of persons in pastoral care and counseling. The potential of the vitality and witness of today's liturgical reform extends to the free churches—including evangelicals—and their pastoral ministries. The revised rite of reconciliation in the Roman Catholic Church, for example, seems far closer to being the practical and pastoral application of Luther's doctrine of justification by faith than what one finds going on in much of Protestant ministry today. Of course, being receptive to liturgical reform as a source of pastoral and personal renewal does not demand submission to the hegemony of all liturgical assumptions.

In addition, a renewed interest in Christian spirituality (or piety, to use the term proper in the Reformed tradition) is noteworthy in churches, seminaries, and pastoral care training centers. Many in mainline churches who fled a piety that for them no longer had meaning have found some of the grander promises of a secularist outlook, including psychology, to be barren, and so have returned to spirituality with a new perspective. They are, of course, wary of pietism, self-conscious piety for its own sake, or anything that seeks escape from life rather than renewal for living. The reality of the Transcendent One, however, beckons and haunts. Some way to come to terms with the persistent call of God and to rejuvenate Christian faith and ministry is the order of the day.

Of course, both the modern pastoral care movement and the liturgical reform movement, like many renewal movements, contain elements of a sectarian mind-set. Observe the special vocabularies, cliques, and new orthodoxies in each. These, however, are not the essential qualities or thrusts of either current pastoral care or worship.

RELIGIOUS RENEWAL OF MINISTRY

As a free church minister, then, I look toward reform in worship, a process now quite ecumenical, as a source of renewal for a diverse group of ministers committed to pastoral care and counseling ministry. In liturgical churches, the explicitly sacramental basis is "the effective means of grace in pastoral care."[3] John Donne represents sacramental pastoral care: "If you have truly given yourself to him in the Sacrament, God has given you yourself back so much mended as that you have received yourself and him too."[4] To appropriate such sources, however, does not necessitate taking a strictly liturgical or sacramental view of pastoral care. Prayer may be

3. William H. Peterson, "On the Pattern and in the Power: A Historical Essay of Anglican Pastoral Care," in James E. Griffiss, ed., *Anglican Theology and Pastoral Care* (Wilton, Conn.: Morehouse-Barlow, 1985), 17.

4. John Donne, *The Showing Forth of Christ: Sermons of John Donne*, ed. Edmund Fuller (New York: Harper and Row, 1964), 79.

liturgical or free, and I believe it is the foremost consideration in pastoral care as embodied in both types of church tradition. Prayer is one of the basic forms of responding to God's love and grace and of offering our-selves—including our ministries of care—to God.

To put forward the idea that contemporary liturgical renewal is a source of renewal in pastoral ministry is not to claim that the former is the answer to all problems of substance in pastoral care. In fact, one of the limitations of current liturgical reform is the widespread tendency to define "pastoral liturgy" simply as an answer to the needs of people. In other words, the questions come out of the life of the people, and the liturgy is a responsive answer to these problems. Like Tillich's method of correlation, this per-spective is one-sided.

Although the thesis of this book does not assume a liturgical under-standing of pastoral care, it does advocate a religious model of pastoral care. What undergirds pastoral care in essence, if not in all of its expres-sions, is religious and theological. If the substructure is religious, then religious forms of expression ought to be natural and not uncommon. Such an assumption does not infer that pastoral care has not learned much from secular disciplines or that pastoral care does not have much more to learn from these disciplines. Learning from them, however, is far different from the tendency in much of contemporary pastoral care to model ministry on the norms and ways of secular healing. The cure of souls is one thing. Psychodynamic finesse, although it can contribute to the cure of souls, is quite another. In the process of learning from psychodynamic perspectives, pastoral counselors, chaplains, and others inevitably have become fasci-nated with this culturally alive source of understanding. The techniques of free association, dream interpretation, and so on are in fact interminable (for example, there is no proper place to end free association except when the arbitrarily structured "hour" is up) and generate endless theories to illuminate the process. Hence, "The tree dies under the hungry weight of the vines."[5]

Pastoral Care as Religious Action

To claim that pastoral care is religious is to call for a reexamination of how pastoral counselors and pastors have positioned themselves in relation to other helping professions, their practices, and their language of self-understanding. Which is the first habit of pastors and pastoral coun-selors—to pray and reflect prayerfully on their caring, or to analyze their countertransferences?

5. George Steiner, *Real Presences: Is There Anything in What We Say?* (London: Faber, 1989), 45–47.

In raising this question and positing that pastoral care ministry is basically religious action and requires religious language, I am not calling for the expulsion of secular language. The liturgy already has plenty of that, and so does most theology. To call for such exclusion might support the mistaken assumption that prayer is relevant only for explicitly religious life and action. The point is rather that secular language alone cannot do justice to the action encountered in the liturgy or in pastoral care and counseling. Secular language and the perspectives of secular disciplines often are helpful in understanding pastoral ministry; religious language always is essential. The latter is essential because the authority of pastors and pastoral counselors does not derive properly from their knowledge of psychological theory or skills, but adheres to their role as listeners to and representative voices of Christian faith.

In short, the kind of examination of prayer and other forms of ritual in pastoral care proposed here should be of interest to a number of people: pastors and others who want to reflect on their own ambivalence regarding prayer and the way in which this dynamic shapes their pastoral care and counseling; specialists in pastoral care and counseling who seek a perspective that can anchor their practice in a pastoral theology that maintains conversation with contemporary secular disciplines but at the same time opens up lively dialogue with Christian tradition and theology; and persons in the free church traditions who have a high appreciation for the place of religious resources in pastoral ministry and also are ready to reexamine their practice critically in light of other religious traditions, especially because these have been undertaking their reform on the basis of biblical study and evangelical interest.

THE PURPOSE OF PASTORAL CARE

If the liturgical renewal movement—insofar as it restores and revitalizes the prayer life of the people and the means of grace of the church—does in fact have the kind of impact on the practice of pastoral care that I anticipate, then it will become clear that the prayers, formal and informal, of the community of faith establish the spirit of all pastoral care. According to the Roman Catholic "Apostolic Letter on the Sacred Liturgy," the purpose of Vatican II's Constitution on the Sacred Liturgy is to lead the faithful to "an active celebration of the mysteries."[6] Even if one's tradition is non-liturgical, one can still see that the purpose of pastoral care is much the same—participation in the mysteries of God in our midst and the celebration of the gospel of Christ.

6. Quoted in *Southwark Liturgy Bulletin* 68 (July 1989): 1.

MEANS OF GRACE IN RENEWAL

The means of grace are ways to encounter the God of transcendence, order, and freedom—ways that are explicitly set aside, designated, and tried-and-true. Such means of grace impose no limit on God—God gives God's grace in countless ways. Yet, over the generations the people of God have come to affirm particular ways of waiting for God, ways not to be neglected. Also, these designated ways serve as paradigms for the innumerable ways in which God gives gifts. Prayer can be considered as the first means of grace. As prayer is a "special exercise of faith," so every means of grace is an exercise of faith.[7] Faith works in means of grace such as prayer, Scripture (read, preached, studied, heard deeply in meditation), and sacraments or ordinances of the church. Faith draws persons to these means of grace as faith lures them to God. Further, the exercise of faith through these means of grace strengthens this God-given faith.

Usually, those who place much emphasis on the official means of grace in any tradition envision the work of the Holy Spirit as being orderly and structured.[8] John Wesley, however, is representative of those who endeavor to combine high appreciation for the means of grace and an emphasis on radical inner transformation. Rosemary Haughton highlights the contrast by stating that transformation results from the conflict of grace and formation. The latter refers to a set of values represented in the structures of a well-ordered community and personal life. The former brings about the unimaginable and cannot be contained in structures. In Haughton's view, formation is good and is necessary to and a preparation process for transformation, but it is also potentially suffocating and erodes awareness of the need for grace. Further, she also acknowledges that transformation results from a conflict between grace and evil.[9] Others stress that transformation is known by the encounter of a "power not ourselves," whereas formation is marked with the traces of our own management. Perhaps a third term should not be excluded—*reformation,* a forming once again, a kind of renewing return to original faith and practice with a difference. *Reform* is a mediate term; it refers neither to simple progression (a notion implicit in formation) nor to the virtual annihilation of the old with the onslaught of the new (implicit in the notion of transformation). Usually, however, reform has an institution or movement as its object. At the personal level a different phrase often is used: the amendment of life.

7. Martin Luther, "Treatise on Good Works," in Theodore G. Tappert, ed., vol. 1 of *Selected Writings of Martin Luther* (Philadelphia: Fortress Press, 1967), 140.
8. James E. Griffiss, "Theology and Pastoral Care," in *Anglican Theology,* 93, 94.
9. Rosemary Haughton, *The Transformation of Man: A Study of Conversion and Community* (Paramus, N.J.: Paulist Press, 1967).

However such issues are worked through, it is the grace of God that is received through these means. No attitude or claim that detracts from a sense of free grace is appropriate to the means of grace.

The representation of God in one's mental life is powerfully bonded to one's perception of self.[10] Consequently, it is plausible to anticipate that any basic alteration in self-understanding results in a changed understanding of God, and that any basic change in one's vision of God alters one's own self-concept. The various forms of psychotherapy usually focus on changing self-concept. This is one way of bringing about a difference in one's experience of God. In contrast, one might consider that the church's means of grace are ways of focusing on the formation or transformation of one's vision of God, and thus of bringing about a difference in one's self-understanding.

Spiritual Renewal in Practice

This book is an initial exploration into select means of grace in the life and tradition of the church. The topics covered are prayer, *lectio divina* (divine reading, or meditation on Scripture), reconciliation (or confession/absolution), baptism, and Holy Communion or Eucharist. Although far from a complete list of the means of grace, these topics are salient in any ministry of word and sacrament, or any ministry that gives attention to ordinances.

The procedure followed generally in this study is to approach each topic theologically. This first, theological interpretation of the text is followed by a psychological analysis as a way of reconsidering the topic or repositioning the liturgical text being examined so that it speaks clearly to the personal situations encountered in pastoral care ministry. Certain images draw persons close to primary relationships as preserved in memory and kept alive in mental life, whether these mental representations of relationships are life-affirming or threatening. Such images of primary relationships reflect the context in which one's self-image was born and help maintain one's self-understanding. Attentiveness to these personal images of primary relationships will help us to read liturgical texts and their metaphors in relation to the dynamics of pastoral care events beyond public worship, and this in turn will help in relocating and marking a new position for liturgical texts from which dialogue can ensue.

The analysis results in a discussion of the implications of theological and psychological understanding for the practice of pastoral care. The

10. Frazer Watts and Mark Williams, *The Psychology of Religious Knowing* (Cambridge: Cambridge University Press, 1988), 35.

practical consequences of the interpretation are not simple applications; for example, the theological and psychological analysis of baptism does not conclude with a discussion limited to how the analysis applies to baptism ministry. Instead, the analysis of baptism issues in a discussion of practical implications for all pastoral care. In principle, the kind of analysis undertaken with the topics of this study can be employed with other sacraments or ordinances.

LIVING HUMAN TEXTS

Pastoral theology in its most elemental form is rooted in disciplined observation of pastoral ministry. As the etymological image behind the word *theory* is the deed of witness by legates sent to observe the oracles and rites at the sacred Attic games, so pastoral theology is grounded in the patient observation that enables one to testify to what takes place and interpret it. In former times such observation has been embodied in model texts, such as the Puritan "cases of conscience." Today we have revived the case method and also examine verbatim reports of pastoral visits and counseling sessions. One of the assumptions of this book is that both liturgical texts and pastoral records can be understood as observations of pastoral ministry. The task undertaken in this book is not to present a complete method for doing pastoral theology, which would entail a complicated "dialogue" of two different kinds of texts. This book rather attempts to disclose the importance of means of grace in pastoral care by moving from our common worship to pastoral care and counseling situations.

Anton Boisen saw the hermeneutics of great lives (actually the lives of common people when they faced critical issues—in Boisen's situation, the mentally ill who faced crises and deep, religious issues bravely) in analogy to the hermeneutics of the great books of the Christian faith (Christian classics). Accordingly he advocated that ministers' interactions with individuals be recorded in case form. In his setting, the mental hospital, such "living human documents," which were to be "read in the original,"[11] became texts for deeper pastoral and personal understanding, and the patient became the chaplain's teacher. This was a creative proposal, but it was used only to justify pastoral theology as reflection via cases, not to inaugurate a dialogue between these "texts"—that is, between Christian classics and contemporary ministry events. Nor did Boisen specify a method for interpreting "living human documents" in the direction of Scripture and classics of Christian tradition, other than to propose that a theological question be put to the cases examined.

11. Anton T. Boisen, *Problems in Religion and Life: A Manual for Pastors* (New York: Abingdon-Cokesbury Press, 1946), 38.

THE CLASSIC TEXTS OF THE CHURCH

The text that represents the immediacy of pastoral experience, however, is not the only text to be examined in pastoral theology. Scripture and theology provide "classic" texts that inform and shape pastoral ministry and guide disciplined reflection on it. Careful exegesis of these texts contributes to careful "exegesis" of case studies and verbatim reports. Likewise, careful observation of ministry experiences contributes to careful observation of Scripture and other theological texts. Liturgical texts have the advantage of occupying a middle ground: They shape pastoral ministry so concretely that they give a report of what happens, and at the same time they are texts that use Scripture and distill theological understanding. In this book, which focuses on means of grace, liturgical texts are the "classical" source for reflection. The texts used in this book are not "classical" in a literal sense, for they are contemporary. Yet, these texts are interpretations of Scripture and theological classics, and thus can be called classic insofar as they are faithful to Scripture and the theological classics of Christian faith.

In one sense, a complete pastoral theology is constructed out of an ongoing dialogue between two very different kinds of texts, theological texts and pastoral records (or "living human documents"). But can one simply set two different kinds of texts side by side? To do so literally is unwieldy and unworkable. There is no simple correlation or direct translation of one into the other. So how are the two to be related?

The differences between the two kinds of texts highlight the problem. A liturgical text reflects the work of many persons and trials, a process that eventuates in acceptance and standardization. It is a text that endures, a text slowly and carefully formed, and one that resists impulsive change. The pastoral record tries to capture the spontaneity of the moment, is hastily constructed in the transition between acts, and usually is "fixed" as a text only for brief consultation with professional colleagues. Such texts are the first fruits of pastoral ministry, while liturgical texts are the final harvest of a season in the history of God's people. The liturgy intends to include all the people, even though it can fail significantly. The pastoral record is idiosyncratic, insisting on the uniqueness of the individual and the particular. The language of the liturgy, even new liturgies, is not ordinary speech, but uncommon speech for common people. The case study or verbatim report, in contrast, is common speech, but the insights it provokes seem rarely destined for all people. The liturgy protects the purity of the church; the pastoral record shows how often such purity is set aside, if only momentarily, to guard the integrity and the ego of the individual, whether parishioner or pastor. The liturgical and the pastoral texts, the public and personal moments of pastoral ministry, each inherently contains probing questions for the other, making inevitable a mutual cross-examination.

THE DIALOGUE OF THE TWO TEXTS

Can these two texts forgive each other their faults and be at table together?

Actually, the differences between these two types of texts mark out the distance between them, a distance that creates the space for dialogue. Some process of ongoing dialogue between these two sources for pastoral theology is vital to any specific method. Furthermore, particular, common features of these texts are telling. They reveal a boundary that holds the two in some proximity. Each kind of text represents an event of ministry, events that however different belong together as part of one ministry. Both kinds of texts are replete with symbols and metaphors that express the spirit and strike the heart, for both embody theological interpretations and pastoral self-understanding. Both are brimming with the fullness of life before God. We can read through the text of a Eucharist liturgy, but we cannot treat this text as the real event, although it represents the real event. Every service of the Eucharist is a "performance" of this ritual, a performance that interprets its meaning much as a musician's performance interprets a musical masterpiece. Consequently, although the liturgy as a text stays the same, each time worship takes place the liturgy undergoes a new interpretation. In a similar manner, each act of pastoral care is a performance of the meaning of caring, a rendering into being, a response to deep-seated convictions and prayer.

This book responds to the question of how the two texts are related by following the trail of another question: How is a liturgical text to be analyzed in the direction of pastoral care? It is beyond the scope of this introductory work, then, to exhibit an explicit dialogue between liturgical texts and pastoral records, although the habit of analyzing both kinds of texts influences the analysis and discussion here. This book does show a way of reading liturgical texts for guidance in pastoral care. After all, a liturgical text is pastoral care frozen in time in the sense that it represents God's care for human beings and juxtaposes in one event reverence for God and being pastors one to another.

Most of the ensuing chapters make use of liturgical texts, which are quoted extensively. In addition to the fact that these texts may not be readily available to some readers, their presentation within these chapters allows the texts to speak for themselves.

In the perspectival approach of Seward Hiltner, the inductive approach was to lead to theological reflection and conclusions. In contrast, Derek Tidball says, "The shepherding perspective may well inform and question the theology but more fundamentally the theology will inform and question the work of the shepherd and that relationship must not be reversed."[12] As set up thus far, however, such a debate leads nowhere. Insofar as the liturgical text and the pastoral record represent different moments in ministry, theological construction and arguments from both can and should appeal to Scripture, Christian tradition, reason, and the Spirit. In reflecting on the means of grace in both types of texts, pastors make contact with the mysterious reality that surrounds their ministry, a contact that should be as carefully reasoned as possible even though the process is not limited to theory or rationality.

---

12. Derek J. Tidball, *Skillful Shepherds: An Introduction to Pastoral Theology* (Downers Grove, Ill.: InterVarsity Press, 1986), 24.

CHAPTER 1

Prayer: The Soul

Pastoral care ministry pays little attention to prayer these days. Not that no one prays in the course of caring for others; rather, little attention is given to what caregivers are doing when they pray, to the decision whether or not to pray with persons, and to the relation between one's own prayer discipline as a pastor or representative of Christian faith and the way one does pastoral care. Pastors can consult with specialists in pastoral care and counseling, but little or no attention will be given to prayer.

This could suggest that pastors are so confident about prayer and their knowledge of prayer that little analysis and reflection are needed. My experience among students and clergy, however, suggests otherwise.

Two observations can lend greater insight regarding this lacuna. First, prayer often is viewed as part of ritual behavior—a part of what is expected of clergy when ministering in the presence of others. When viewed as routine, prayer hardly seems worth special examination. Second, prayer is connected with a particular but often unspoken attitude. Persons whose self-understanding and world orientation are shaped largely by modern psychological thought usually view prayer as a form of self-talk. As such prayer has power to alter one's attitude, but like all self-talk needs no particular attention or method of analysis. So it is no surprise that in Clinical Pastoral Education, for example, one rarely sees a verbatim report of a pastoral visit wherein a prayer receives the same attention as the human conversation. The reason for the neglect of reflection on prayer in pastoral care is not that such specialists have become well-versed in psychological literature. Rather this neglect is caused largely by certain cultural trends and core assumptions that virtually permeate our culture. Accordingly, the lack of attention to prayer is not characteristic merely of specialists in pastoral care and counseling. Others who are less articulate psychologically may not voice this view in psychological jargon, but they operate out of the same perspective: Prayer is self-talk. The influence of existentialism is a living source of this cultural habit of mind: The unknowability of God—the divine nonobjectifiability—issues in theological statements that refer to human existence and self-understanding. With respect to pastoral ministry, prayer is assumed implicitly and at times overtly to be self-talk. No wonder that prayer is viewed as less important than genuine dialogue and dynamic interaction between persons.

Along with this cultural dimension of the problem one has to acknowledge a personal and existential dimension. At times, when I have talked with pastors and chaplains about their views of God and prayer, I have asked the question: What do you resent about God? Many times the same response has been given (and it is my response as well): The silence! This is the expression of ministers who have been present to people in their griefs and crises, who with them have felt that absence of God, the very God these clergy are committed to represent. Although their compassion for these suffering persons was real enough, their prayers were empty, and seemed misplaced when the Other did not appear to be there. That is, emotionally prayer was experienced as self-talk, not communion with God the Other.

A Theology of Sacred Space

In response to the ambivalence regarding prayer, I shall argue that even from a psychological perspective, prayer may not simply be self-talk. Moreover, I shall advance the thesis that prayer is the soul of pastoral care, and that it is time to give prayer central place in pastoral theory as well as practice. This means that pastoral theology's major challenge is to construct a viable and valid understanding of prayer in the practice of pastoral care. Such an understanding is essential if the inherent connectedness of pastoral care and counseling to the public ministry of the church is to be discerned.

Prayer will be understood here simply as human communication with God. From the human side, this means that prayer will be viewed as mental activity that has God or a divine image as its object, direct or indirect. Although far too narrow for some, especially those who want everything to be called prayer, this definition establishes an identifiable field of study. Its theological problems (for example, God is always subject, not object) and psychological problems (What is the locus of the divine image?) will be discussed later. As human communication with God, prayer takes many forms: public or liturgical prayer, personal devotions in time set aside from daily tasks, and "prayer without ceasing" (or a prayer such as the Jesus Prayer repeated constantly throughout the day when one's mind is not taken up with other activity that demands complete concentration).

By "soul" here I mean that prayer is of the inner essence of pastoral care practice—its essence is prayer, its destiny prayerfulness. An understanding of the place of prayer in pastoral care, I maintain, is necessary to an understanding of the fundamental purpose and aims of pastoral care, its functions, and its structure. If prayer is the soul of pastoral care, then the task of pastoral theology is to discern how prayer is embodied and given expression in any act of pastoral ministry.

THE IMPORTANCE OF CELEBRATION

The best-known current definition of pastoral care is that of Clebsch and Jaekle, cited above. That definition; once again, is this: "The ministry of the cure of souls, or pastoral care, consists of helping acts, done by *representative Christian persons,* directed toward the *healing, sustaining, guiding, and reconciling of troubled persons* whose troubles arise in *the context of ultimate meanings and concerns.*"[1] I believe that celebration is just as much a basic function of pastoral care as are the four functions highlighted by Clebsch and Jaekle. Somehow, the use of the shepherding image has narrowed the understanding of the nature of pastoral care. Pastoral care has come to mean caring for persons when they, like sheep, are lost or sick. But the work of a shepherd includes oversight of sheep's normal life and daily feeding as well.

In my first visit to Europe—which included cities and towns such as St. Gall, Bern and Lucerne in Switzerland, and Salzburg in Austria—I gained a new interpretation for the meaning of the term *pastoral.* These and numerous other cities I visited were, for me, pastoral. I realized that the word *pastoral* should not have exclusively rural connotations. These towns and cities were pastoral in that they provided space for human activity—space that in some ways resembled a pasture. In marketplaces and courtyards, where motor traffic was excluded, people gathered and walked around. Some sat and ate and drank. Some simply watched what other people did. Still others listened to live music played on a corner. Some gazed at the artistic design and decoration of old buildings. Time was not a rushing stream; it slowed to a calm flow brimming with life. Here, a way of enjoying life seemed provided for and effortless. This, too, is a dimension of pastoral care. Pastoral care is person-centered and not necessarily problem-oriented. To be pastoral includes being with people

---

1. William A. Clebsch and Charles R. Jaekle, *Pastoral Care in Historical Perspective: An Essay with Exhibits* (Englewood Cliffs, N.J.: Prentice-Hall, 1964), 4.

in their celebrations and daily living.

For a revised working definition of pastoral care, then, consider the following: The ministry of pastoral care consists of service done by representative Christian persons, directed toward the celebrating, healing, sustaining, guiding, and reconciling of persons whose joys and troubles arise in the context of ultimate meanings.

This revision opens the way to considering that if prayer is the soul of pastoral care, then the corporate worship of the church is the primary context from which pastoral care draws its life—its vitality and its purpose. As worship includes celebrating, healing, sustaining, guiding, and reconciling through the grace of God discovered in the gathered community of faith, so pastoral care facilitates these ministries with persons beyond the "sacred space" of public worship. Although the focus of pastoral care is on the personal and interpersonal worlds, it is appropriate to begin an analysis of prayer in relation to pastoral care by examining prayer in corporate worship.

THE NEED FOR SACRED SPACE

The concept of sacred space is essential for an understanding of the place of prayer in public worship. Mircea Eliade believed that profane space is homogeneous, is without gaps and interruptions, lacks creativity, has no center for orientation, and is the locus of deterioration. For him sacred space or a religious orientation introduces heterogeneity:

> For religious man, space is not homogeneous; he experiences interruptions, breaks in it; some parts of space are qualitatively different from others. "Draw not nigh hither," says the Lord to Moses; "put off thy shoes from off thy feet, for the place whereon thou standest is holy ground" (Exod. 3:5). There is, then, a sacred space, and hence a strong, significant space; there are other spaces that are not sacred and so are without structure or consistency, amorphous. Nor is this all. For religious man, this spatial nonhomogeneity finds expression in the experience of an opposition between space that is sacred—the holy *real* and *real-ly* existing space—and all other space, the formless expanse surrounding it.[2]

For Eliade sacred space is anchored in the absolute in a way that profane space is not. Sacred space provides access to the primordial and creative. The boundary between sacred space and profane space is very important. One moves from one to the other very carefully.

Victor Turner elaborated on this concept in terms of "liminality." For him rites of passage involve at least three phases: separation, transition,

2. Mircea Eliade, *The Sacred and the Profane: The Nature of Religion,* (New York: Harper and Row, 1961), 26.

and incorporation or reaggregation. Separation is the movement across the border from profane to sacred space. Transition or liminality is one's state in sacred space because one has left behind all statuses and ordinary ways of thinking. Incorporation is actually a reincorporation into what might be called ordinary consciousness.[3]

In genuine worship people cross this boundary described by anthropologists and historians of religion—a boundary that marks off another space. In worship people enter another world, a sacred world that transcends profane life and transforms those who enter it.

The sanctuary is sacred space. Although people can discover the sacred anywhere, "sacred space" is not merely a catchy phrase designating an inner attitude. Rather, the inner attitude arises in an environment. A particular setting evokes awareness of the sacred. Of course, a particular place might do this for one person but not for another. So we might say that sacred space is an interaction of the outer and the inner or is a fusion of the two. A sanctuary has been designated, usually publicly, by a community of people as a sacred place, a place where people cross the boundary from the profane to the sacred. Designated as a sacred place, the sanctuary is designed to serve in this way. Its shape, materials, and symbolic objects mark it as a distinctive place.

Entering the designated sacred place and allowing it to become true sacred space require preparation. In a general sense, all of a community's and a person's past life is preparation for this moment. More immediately, preparation includes the day preceding worship and the transitional preparations for worship leading up to its beginning. The Episcopalian Collect for Saturdays directs attention to such preparation:

> Almighty God, who after the creation of the world didst rest from all thy works and sanctify a day of rest for all thy creatures: Grant that we, putting away all earthly anxieties, may be duly prepared for the service of thy sanctuary, and that our rest here upon earth may be a preparation for the eternal rest promised to thy people in heaven; through Jesus Christ our Lord. Amen.[4]

In a sanctuary people gather in silence or listen to a musical prelude, or both. Also, in most worship services a hymn is sung at or very near the beginning. Music and silence are primary ways in which people prepare themselves to worship and begin to worship. They become involved in acts and attitudes that surpass ordinary cognition. Their bodily behavior

3. Victor Turner, *From Ritual to Theatre: The Human Seriousness of Play* (New York; Performing Arts Journal Publications, 1982).

4. *The Book of Common Prayer* (New York: Church Hymnal Corporation and Seabury Press, 1977), 56.

facilitates and expresses this fact. In standing or kneeling, for example, they assume postures that symbolize inner attitudes. It is not enough for one to think privately that one has these attitudes, they must be acted out and embodied.

To begin worshiping introduces a dynamic tension: The worshipers are not always aware of God's presence, and so they intentionally "enter" that presence. They do not always believe, but in prayer they begin to believe again. They forget their baptism, but in worship, they remember once again. They are not always a community as they are meant to be, but they gather together and are made a community in spite of everything. They stand in need of salvation and reconciliation. They come into God's presence to recognize the nearness of God and receive these favors. In everyday life their tendency perhaps is to be but dimly and vaguely aware of God, but here the practice is to speak of God in concrete ways: Almighty God, Lord Jesus Christ, Holy Spirit.

A typical beginning of worship has the leader call the people to worship, usually with a sentence or two from Sacred Scripture. A mutual greeting follows, such as:

LEADER: The Lord be with you.
PEOPLE: And with thy spirit.

Another common beginning is a mutual prayer:

LEADER: O Lord, open thou our lips.
PEOPLE: And our mouth shall show forth thy praise.

With such words the leader and the people pray for each other, in effect blessing each other, or they join in prayer. The mutual greeting is a prayer, but one not addressed directly to God; rather it is addressed to one another with reference to God incorporated into the greeting. This prayer focuses on the horizontal, the social relationship, with the explicit intent of opening this relationship up to the transcending presence of God. In some churches there may be differing roles sacramentally; however, in the total context of worship and the community of faith, the people are priests to each other. This is so because in the presence of God this mutuality comes to recognition: God is God and the worshipers are instruments of the divine grace, a grace first received in community. It is by no means insignificant that in the presence of one another worshipers recognize the presence of God, or that in the presence of God they recognize mutuality in their being present to one another.

In Jewish and Christian traditions, the reality and presence of God are bound up with a sense of community. Consequently, in these traditions personal prayer and prayer in pastoral care are bonded to this communal framework. For Jews and Christians alike the personal experience of sacred space is organically related to the communal experience of sacred space.

As a way of entering sacred space, prayer brings together the inner and outer, the personal and social, the human and the transcendent. Because of this prayer is often thought of as the first means of grace.

PRAYER AS A MEANS OF GRACE

To speak of prayer as a means of grace is to place prayer in the Christian context and its traditions. Thus prayer is considered in light of particular histories, including histories of interpreting the meaning and place of prayer in relation to the means and ways of grace. In Christian tradition a major tension balances the practice of prayer: the tension between the *kataphatic* (Gk.: make clear, visible, plain) and the *apophatic* (Gk: denial, negation). Public prayer is the starting point of my analysis, and particular attention will be given to the images and metaphorical language of prayer. Consequently, this analysis does not do justice to the mystical *via negativa* (negative way) in relation to pastoral care. Rather, the approach taken here maintains prayer within the God/people and God/person framework and does not go beyond this relational perspective into any mysticism in which self is annihilated. The annihilation of self and the absence of God, as examined in this book, are aspects of a community's and a subject's journey of faith where images of God, self, and others are in the process of being transformed.

In his book on prayer, Karl Barth says that the question the reformers addressed was: "How is it possible for me to have an encounter with God?" Barth proclaims that this is the question the minister hopes to deal with in every pastoral relationship. Barth's theology answers the question by stating that this encounter is possible because Jesus Christ is our representative before God and by Jesus Christ humanity is placed in the presence of God. Within this framework, Barth sees prayer as a "necessary and essential act, which must come by itself."[5] It comes by itself because it proceeds from Christ's praying for us; it proceeds from a grace by which God tells us how to pray and for what to pray. Barth's emphasis is not on prayer as a means of grace so much as on prayer as a sign of grace at work. The tension is unavoidable: prayer as God's gift and Christ's ongoing ministry versus prayer as our response to God, a way in which to confidently expect grace from God.

Genuine prayer is given to persons (is not of their own making) in at least two senses: (1) People pray when they cannot do otherwise. Prayers come upon them. Without planning they find themselves praying, whether

5. Karl Barth, *Prayer,* 2d ed. (Philadelphia: Westminster Press, 1985), 24.

rarely or often. The Spirit, like wind, blows where it will (John 3:8). Being of the Spirit, true prayer comes and goes of its own accord and cannot be regulated or produced according to a formula. The Lord's Prayer is no formula. Guidelines for prayer in pastoral ministry are not set out as formulas or as a means of dictating the orthodox way to pray. Rather than emphasizing the guidelines themselves, the process of their emergence from reflection on liturgy and on pastoral experience should be noted for the development of prayer in one's own ministry. (2) People pray out of such deeply entrenched habit that to do so is essential to their sense of who they are and what they are about. Prayer is like breathing or like one's daily work that affirms one's sense of identity—the work may not be easy but helps define what one is.

Character development and personal transformation are fundamental issues in current studies of human behavior. What, then, is the place of the means of grace, and prayer in particular, in the processes of formation and transformation in one's life before God? The "Apostolic Letter on the Sacred Liturgy" states that the most urgent of the church's tasks is "biblical and liturgical formation of the people of God, both pastors and faithful."[6] Here *formation* is an inclusive term that refers to the lifelong process of growth in the grace of God. Because there are different kinds of experiences in this journey of faith—events that flow continuously from one to another with gradual change and some that erupt out of life and introduce discontinuity—both *formation* and *transformation* are important terms in this study. Louis Weil emphasizes how fundamental formation is to the task of pastoral care. For him, formation involves knowledge of the church's faith, participation in worship, a life of prayer, and commitment to service.[7]

To raise the question of character formation and personal transformation is to raise the question of the relation between liturgical transformation in sacred space and transformation in daily living. I recognize that some persons maintain a sufficiently rigid separation between the two that public worship does not seem to be related to changes outside of worship. Yet for others, dynamic, pervasive, and stable change flows from the life of prayer. That is, public worship and personal prayer for them sustain a continuous process of transformation whereby all of life becomes a prayer to God. For them participation in sacred space is the key to transformation in all places.

If sacred space can transform all of life, then any bifurcation of worship and ethics is mistaken. If worship is the church "doing its identity,"[8] then

6. Quoted in *Southwark Liturgy Bulletin* 68 (July 1989): 1.
7. Louis Weil, "Worship and Pastoral Care," in James E. Griffiss, ed., *Anglican Theology and Pastoral Care* (Wilton, Conn.: Morehouse-Barlow, 1985), 122–28.
8. Ibid., 116

the essential act of faith is oblation or offering, and the prayer of faith enables practical and intelligent commitment to service and justice. Louis Weil summarizes the inherent relation between prayer and ethics in this manner: "Pastoral care is the inevitable service of a worshipping community that has embraced the full dimensions of the symbols of faith. A liturgical mentality that is turned in on itself . . . is perverse. It fails to undertake the lifestyle, our incorporation with others, that the rites are called to articulate."[9] Cyprian stated that prayer without alms is barren; although that may sound a bit quaint, it puts the matter concisely.[10]

I have acknowledged that there are risks in an approach to Christian life and ministry that centers on religious resources such as prayer; however, there are also risks in approaches that center on ethics. All too commonly the latter will lean toward either moralism or rationalism, and so either contradict the gospel or offer clarity without motivational power. Still, although I believe that prayer is the soul of pastoral care and theology, it is not the only subject, and the "superstructures" of caring service and ethical choices must receive their full due. R. D. Laing has said that "among physicians and priests, there should be some who are guides, who can educt the person from this world and induct him to another."[11] Laing, then, would seem to be emphasizing the trancendent aspect of ministry and prayer. In contrast, Daniel Berrigan has stated that at the political level, prayer and contemplation are "deeply subversive activities."[12] Berrigan, then, emphasizes how ethical choices and action issue from prayer. The issue for pastoral ministry becomes how prayer can result in the manifestation of grace both within prayer itself and in the wider world of ethical decisions.

GOD'S PRESENCE AND ABSENCE

Prayer has practical consequences; however, prayer is a way of waiting for God, and the worship of God is not to be justified merely by other ends that are well served in the process. To understand prayer as sacred space and as the soul of pastoral care, we need a theme that discloses the essential interrelationship between the communal and the personal. I believe that God's presence and absence in human experience is such a theme, one that generates genuine dialogue between corporate prayer and the dynamics of pastoral care. The presence and absence of God is the hermeneutical theme that opens liturgy to pastoral theology.

9. Ibid., 119.
10. Quoted in Joseph A. Jungmann, *Christian Prayer through the Centuries* (New York: Paulist Press, 1978), 10.
11. R. D. Laing, *The Politics of Experience and the Bird of Paradise* (Harmondsworth, England: Penguin, 1967), 136.
12. Daniel Berrigan, *America Is Hard to Find* (London: SPCK, 1973), 77, 78.

The presence of God is a fundamental theme in the Old and New Testaments. Samuel Terrien argues that this theme pervades and holds these Scriptures together, elucidating the integrity of the canon.[13] The presence of God is perhaps *the* theme of the Psalms, for example. It is hardly surprising, then, that this theme is vital to all Christian worship. Certainly it is central to understanding prayer.

The beginnings of corporate worship consistently address the theme of the presence of God. The greeting "The Lord be with you" is an example, but how can one presume to speak so boldly and specifically about the presence of God? Those at worship are not better than others. The cares of daily life distract and preoccupy them as much as others. It is as if, in the invocation of God's presence, something were being hidden, denied, or placed in the background. In a way, the reality being denied is the experience of the absence of God. Should not the absence of God be held in dynamic tension with faith in God's presence? In the beginnings of worship this denial seems to be intentional; it is part of the blind leap of faith. So, at the beginning of worship, those present may feel unprepared or disinclined to worship, and they may seem plagued with a sense of the absence of God. In spite of the frequency of this subjective mood, those at worship invoke and proclaim the divine presence. The liturgy, then, conceals, but not completely, a gap between faith and experience, a tension between the presence and absence of God. The beginning of worship does not simply pick up at the point where ordinary experience leaves off. In worship, faith often steps out and stands over against such experience and begins to tell it wonders undreamed of by ordinary consciousness.

If faith leaps beyond momentary subjective feeling in this beginning movement of worship, it does so, in a sense, by leaping back, by imagining life within the larger horizon, not confined to immediate experience—life in light of a saga of faith. Of course, faith also imagines life in terms of the future—in terms of the promises of God that are to be received with confidence as about to reach fulfillment. Perhaps it is better to say simply that the leap of faith repositions worshipers, sets them in a new location of the spirit from where they can envision the wider horizons of their past and future. With reference to their past experience, and not yet introducing the question of the present, those at worship must consider both the presence and the absence of God in their lives. On what basis can they claim that both kinds of experience prepare them for the present moment of encounter with God?

The accent, then, in the opening of worship is on the presence of God. God is present through the representation of Jesus Christ, and God is present

13. Samuel L. Terrien, *The Elusive Presence: The Heart of Biblical Theology* (San Francisco: Harper and Row, 1983).

in the Holy Spirit. Yet, as the Lord's Prayer notes, God is "in heaven"—
not here exactly. Even as present God is a mystery, not known or understood
in the handy ways of a functional approach to life. God is here, and yet
God is not just here. Is it too much to say that God is present and yet God
is absent?

A Psychology of Sacred Space

The above comments suggest not only that a dynamic tension is introduced into consciousness at the beginnings of worship, but also that in this
process worshipers undergo a transition from one frame of mind, including
world orientation and self-understanding, into another. In order to appreciate the significance of this event and to understand the basic experiences
of presence and absence, I want to consider further the concept of sacred
space in psychological terms as a transitional state of mind. In order to do
this I shall shift momentarily from the sacred space of the sanctuary to the
inner "space" of personal thought processes, conscious and unconscious;
and I shall set aside briefly the adult orientation and consider the origins
in infancy of the development of awareness of self and others and the
experience of others' presence and absence.

THE ORIGIN OF SELF AND OTHER

After giving birth, the mother is "overadapted" to the infant; that is,
she is emotionally and physically attuned to the life and needs of the child
in a manner that would be extremely unusual in other relationships. The
mother is often virtually obsessed with the child; the relationship is sym-
biotic. In fact, the interaction of the mother with the child regulates such
phenomena as heart beat and body temperature. This adaptation is so close
that one can infer that initially the infant experiences a magical fusion of
inner wish and outer reality. The paradox is that the infant could not
experience this illusion unless the environment embodied in the mother
makes it possible. The presence of the mother involves caring for biological
needs, playful interaction, and a nondemanding "being there," not trying
to evoke responses from the child, just being near or staying at hand. Of
course, as other members of the family and the mother herself can testify,
many other needs are neglected. As the child grows the mother begins to
become less adaptive to every need of the child, who gradually experiences
frustration. However vaguely or transitorily, impressions of the mother's
otherness begin to dawn on the child. Without such frustration, an awareness
of the mother's otherness, her being a separate person and reality, would
not emerge.

A sense of self is born with these first glimmerings of another. Particularly in the playful interaction between mother and child, the mother

spontaneously imitates the child's behavior—a smile for a smile, and a playful frown for a frown. After a certain amount of biological development and much repetition of this kind of play, the child begins to sense that this imitation is happening and that the mother's face looks like his or her own. That is, the mother is mirroring the child to himself or herself, and the child comes to sense this and gains a first mental image of self by this means. Gradually the image of self is developed in relation to the caring mother and the developing image of her as a separate person. Because of this, self-image is closely tied to the mental image of the primary caring other and the intimate emotional bond represented in these images.

We all are familiar with the phenomenon of the teddy bear or the favored blanket that a child wears out. From a psychological viewpoint, this is a very significant phenomenon, for it reflects the child's use of imagination. Emotionally this is the child's first "possession," and it is not so much the object itself that matters, but the child's use of it. The special object has a personal quality in the young mind. In fact, the object is first used by the child as a way of making present what at times is absent, the caring parent, and so the child clings to the special object as he or she might cling to or touch a parent, and plays with the special object as with a parent. The capacity for symbolic thinking emerges out of infant-mother interaction, so this interaction has been called the child's first culture.[14] A child's capacity for symbolic creativity is greatly strengthened when a mother has spent significant time just being with the child in play or in other interaction that makes no demands on the child.

In other words, when children face the anxiety of transitions—going to sleep, waking, changing from being the focus of the mother's attention to being alone—they soon develop the capacity for a creative solution. An object in the environment takes the place of, or represents, the presence of the mother. This is a clue to a striking mental phenomenon: The child has by then a relatively stable mental image of the mother. That is, she exists in the child's mind as an "object" of experience and thought. Furthermore, the child is learning to let an external object come to symbolize her so that he or she can let her be present even when literally absent.

Because the experience of self originates in relation to the experience of another, this symbol of the other is vital to the ongoing sense of self. The child's creativeness enlarges the child's universe of experience through a playful intermingling of what from an adult viewpoint are inner objects of the mind and outer objects in the environment. We can refer to this phenomenon as the child's "transitional space" and to the symbols the

14. Jerome Bruner, *Actual Minds, Possible Worlds* (Cambridge, Mass.: Harvard University Press, 1986), 114, 115.

child discovers as "transitional objects." For the child such phenomena are neither inside nor outside. In interaction with the transitional object, the child continues to play and discover new aspects of his or her own being. The process serves both defensive functions, enabling one to manage anxiety in face of the absence of the caring other and the unknown, and creative functions, continuing and based on the playful interaction learned in relation to the caring mother.

Just as the child will learn to speak to others, so the child will speak to a mental representation of self, have a dialogue with self. George Herbert Mead envisioned this social structure within the mental life of the person in these terms: The self as subject speaks to the self as object. Thus, the apperception of self as an object endows the self with the same kind of personal qualities that are discovered in the primary others.[15]

Jung and some Jungian therapists tend to envision everything (as in dreams) as part of the self. Images are solipsistic, although projected onto a collective unconscious. Social relations are not worked through except via internal images. But particular images are inherently social. They recapitulate and represent the primordial memories of primary relations, which make up the basic reference points for all other relations. That is, the meaningfulness of all personal relations is constructed with reference to these primary relations out of which the sense of self is born. Ensuing relations may be positive, negative, or mixed, but their energy and subsequently their sense of reality and meaningfulness derive from a connection with the primary images established early in life.

In other words, the very structure of the self is social in its origins, and the very alphabet from which its contents are built up is social in nature.

THE ORIGIN OF MENTAL IMAGES OF GOD

One readily can envision a similarity between the concept of sacred space applied to public prayer above and this new concept of transitional space in the psyche of the child. As sacred space is a place where symbols are used to anchor a community of persons in the divine, so in transitional space the child discovers symbols with which to create a new world located between inner fantasy and outer reality. Now I can proceed to describe how this transitional space becomes sacred for the child by becoming the birthplace for a living, personal, mental representation of the transcendent reality of God.

As the child matures, a host of imaginary mental objects are created, imaginary playmates. Being part of the creative inner life of the child,

---

15. George H. Mead, *Mind, Self and Society from the Standpoint of a Social Behaviorist* (Chicago: University of Chicago Press, 1934). See especially 173–78.

these are part of his or her transitional life; they are transitional "objects" or images whereby the child re-presents external realities and possibilities in the mind.

Usually in the second year of life, a special transitional object becomes a part of the child's life: a mental image of God. This image is based on the mental image of the primary caring person, the mother. The image is a creative synthesis of all kinds of parental qualities, including affective associations. Just as self/other understanding first emerged in the mirroring interaction with the mother, so the relation with God is envisioned in an interpersonal, face-to-face framework. Thus many Psalms speak of God's face. For instance, Psalm 27:8-9 states:

"Come," my heart says, "seek his face!"
Your face, LORD, do I seek.
Do not hide your face from me.

People in every generation speak about God in the same fashion. To cite but one, Simone Weil states: "I only felt in the midst of my suffering the presence of a love, like that which one can read in the smile on a beloved face."[16] In the Psalms and elsewhere the image of a face is used to describe the experience of absence as well as presence. For example, Psalm 88:14 asks:

O LORD, why do you cast me off?
Why do you hide your face from me?

Whereas the mental phenomena of imaginary playmates will fade out of mental life, the mental representation of God endures and is the only "transitional object" to maintain this integral vitality in relation to self-concept. Ana-Maria Rizzuto believes that, at least in Western culture, everyone has a mental representation of God.[17] This mental image of God can be predominantly positive or negative—that is, it can be tied to either a positive or negative sense of self. In adult life aspects of this image of God may be conscious, and much will be retained in unconscious mental life. The original mental representation of God can be added to, or re-worked, as one interacts with others, with culture, and with unpredictable events and crises. Any or all of these can relocate one emotionally back into an in-between or transitional state. From a psychological perspective, this process is a creative one: It is a "construction" that the individual makes out of the phenomena that life presents, especially the personal relationships.

    16. Simone Weil, *Waiting for God,* trans. Emma Graufurd (London: Routledge and Kegan Paul, 1975), 69.
    17. Ana-Maria Rizzuto, *The Birth of the Living God: A Psychoanalytic Study* (Chicago: University of Chicago Press, 1979).

Children construct mental representations of their parents and of themselves. As personal relations develop, one's mental representations of others ordinarily are revised in light of ongoing experience. Sometimes, the mental images prevent perception and understanding of new dimensions in a relationship. It is also worth noting that one can merely think about one's parents when they are absent, but that at times one's thinking seems to provoke an uncanny sense of their presence, although physically they are absent. Although based on the mental representations of parents, the mental representation of God, even in small children's minds, is recognized as referring to reality that is not the same as the parents. It refers, rather, to a wondrous presence that is greater than even the parents. And just as thoughts about parents attempt to reflect one's experience of them, so one's representations of God reflect encounters with this presence. Others' descriptions of God and worship of God affect the child's or the adult's understanding of God.

From a psychogenetic point of view, behind the mental image of God as Father lurks hidden from conscious view the image of God as Mother. Yet the image of God as Father is not merely laid over a deeper, maternal image. Rather, the mother unconsciously conveys an image of the father, who is relatively absent in the sense that he is not virtually always present for the infant as the primary caring person. That is, even while the mother is overadapted to the infant, in the mother's psyche there is present an orientation to a reality other than the child. Later, the child's own image of God is formed out of a creative synthesis of these primary persons as represented in the psyche. Cultural and historical factors account for the dominance of father as the primary, conscious image of God in the thinking of most people. Also, the infant's earliest experiences with the mother are of a piece with the environment, taken for granted and thus not objectified.

Images, suggestions, and events may strike the imagination with force and alter one's concept of God, causing it to transgress the bounds of previous subjective experiencing. But almost always there is a dynamic relationship between the social world, subjective experiences, and mental representations; ordinarily they do not stand still. The hallmark of creative change in religious experience as in all creativity is that childlike sense of experiencing "for the first time ever."

ABSENCE AND A SENSE OF GOD'S REALITY

In the life of young children, a mental representation of God accompanies the symbolic transitional object that represents the bond between parent and self. This image of God evokes the experience of a mysterious presence that holds its own fascination and that comforts in the absence of others. But this mental image does not always bring with it the charged experience of such a presence. Children also experience the absence of their God. Initially, the mental representation of God is not stable. Even as the mysterious presence comes to endure as a mental representation, dwelling in the mind, children encounter the absence of this presence that the mental representation usually evokes. In fact, the absence gives the experience of the mysterious presence an aura of reality; that is, like the parent who becomes real as a separate reality only by being absent and unavailable to fulfill every wish immediately, so God is experienced as other and real psychologically precisely because God is experienced as absent and not as the source of the immediate gratification of every wish.

Always, then, experiences of the absence of God betray a previous presence, a memory or representation that may be conscious or unconscious. That is, without the early experiences of this special transitional object as present there is no possibility of an authentic experience of its absence. The love of God is not always immediately experienced, but love remembered evokes faith. Absence is the clue to presence. As we shall see, the presence of God creates prayer while the absence of God necessitates prayer.

Not only does the absence of God betray some history of the presence of God, but also the absence of God is essential to an authentic sense of the reality of God. The simple reason is that if people experience God as always present and always attending to their well-being, then they have no basis, at least in terms of their experiences, for distinguishing God from fantasy or wish fulfillment.

But does not Christian faith teach that God is everywhere and that God is present always? My point is that this belief is not based on subjective experience, and if it were Christians would have no abiding confidence in the veracity of their claim. This observation about the experience of God's absence is no proof of God's existence, but it does disclose how important this experience is psychologically for a sense of God's reality. Accordingly, Christians believe that God is always present, even though at times they experience the absence of God.

The analogy at the human level already has been mentioned. At the beginning of infants' lives, adult adaptation to them is extremely strong. Adults do whatever is possible to adapt themselves to the infants' needs, but gradually the parents disillusion infants by adapting less to their needs. At the beginning children live in a magic world where it seems that the very cry of need creates the fulfillment of that need, but only incomplete adaptation makes persons real as other persons. That is, persons are experienced as really other precisely because they do not fulfill all our own demands and wishes. When adults remain overadapted to children, children become spoiled and may have limited sensitivity to the reality of others.

Likewise God can be experienced as other than one's own creation precisely because God is experienced as a being who is not always there to satisfy one's wishes. Paradoxically, then, confidence in the reality of God can be supported by the experience of God's absence. Faith points to one who is within, yet who is genuinely other. Although prayer may entail autosuggestion, it transcends autosuggestion in that it involves a real trans-action—communication with God. When one considers the reality of God from the human side, from the viewpoint of our limited experience and understanding, it is evident that the "inner" human story is not a closed circle, is not solipsistic. In prayer the presence of God is experienced as being every bit as real as one's own presence to oneself, yet this is so only because at times one experiences God's absence.

The upshot of this discussion of absence is that absence itself witnesses to the presence of God in human experience, and that absence is vital to confidence in the reality of God.

As children and adults mature, their images of God change. This comes about through contact with family, friends, church, and so on. Such changes often are prompted by experiencing God's absence in transitional periods when one discovers that one's God is "too small" and that one's habitual self-image hosts a false self. Such experiences help prepare the way for a discovery of a more nearly adequate understanding of God, an understand-ing that always is closely bound up with one's own self-image and the process of genuine change in self-image. Just as significant is the fact that any image of God shared by a community of people is closely bound up with that community's self-image. The more nearly mature image of God is not infantile or primitive, but it is primordial.

I have devoted considerable space to describing the transitional object and the emergence of an understanding of God in its earliest form in the human life cycle because this first transition to yield mental concepts of self and other sets the stage for subsequent times of transition in human life: the developmental transitions such as assuming adult status, becoming married, and encountering middle age; and other transitions such as un-anticipated crises. In light of the social and spiritual understanding that is born in early childhood, we can discern more readily what is at stake in the numerous transitions of life that may alter self-understanding and per-sonal relationships, including one's way of relating to God. Furthermore, we now can begin to see how basic are the themes of presence and absence in the personal, interpersonal, and religious dimensions of life. One's first capacities to experience presence and absence are learned through inter-action with a primary caring other, the mother, and are irrevocably tied to one's first mental images of self and others, even one's image of God.

Transitional space is sacred space in the life of the individual from an extremely early age.

The Locus and Referent of Prayer

The sacred spaces of the community and of the person are landscaped and furnished with symbols. Whenever human beings communicate with metaphors, they are close to the realm of prayer. Like poetry in the making, prayer is trying to express the inexpressible. We witness this emphatically when speech becomes difficult, even reduced to silence. But this difficulty is always present. Even in the midst of glib speech, metaphors surface from psychic depths and make their fleeting, cameo appearances, as if under each speech is an underlying text written on the threshold of the unconscious. Perhaps it is too much to claim that this is covert prayer, but the wishes, dreams, loves, beliefs, conflicts, and anomalies that lift up their voices in metaphor and analogy are the material from which are formed much of one's self-understanding in relationship to the divine, the stuff that is destined to become prayer, or at least is meant to become prayer.

In older psychologies such as orthodox psychoanalysis, entering into a transitional frame of mind could be described only as regression. What is constructed internally either may enable an overly defensive distortion of external facts and relationships or may enable a fresh reinterpretation of them. The inner world of mental representations is inhabited by images that both disturb and sustain. In Ibsen's *Ghosts* (1881), Mrs. Alving says, "It isn't what we have inherited from our father and mother that walks in us. It is all kinds of dead ideas and all sorts of old and obsolete beliefs. . . . Inside me it's the dead who live. Ghosts . . . I'm struggling with ghosts— inside and out." Can there not be as well a process whereby new encounters culturally, interpersonally, or biologically open up the possibility of modifying and even transforming deeply internal and old habits of mind and heart—the wild wishes, forbidding ghosts, and guardian angels? In light of the creative character of infantile experience, it must be acknowledged also that this movement of the mind is, at least potentially, creative. The symbol (thought), other (the symbolized), and self form a triangular "space" for the creative activity that enlivens us as human beings.[18] Religion, art, and culture are nurtured and virtually exist in this realm of what is communally and personally transitional: "The assertion of faith is not merely a reassertion of basic trust. . . . It returns to the rudiments of

18. Thomas H. Ogden, "On Potential Space," *International Journal of Psycho-Analysis* 66 (1985): 133.

trust in order to go beyond them. This faith ultimately renounces the imperfection and finitude of basic trust in order to reach beyond it and thereby to recapture it more profoundly."[19] Psychologically, then, the "soul" is one's mental life in a transitional state, the experience of oneself in relation to one's God.

"Transitional" thinking is not simply located inside or outside. It cannot be said, for example, that a child simply "invents" reality for himself or herself. Rather, the child is responding to external stimuli, but in a creative way, so that the external object becomes symbol. This process entails an interaction of internal wish and external reality. Consequently, Don Winnicott and others are led to speak of a "potential space," a realm that lies along or transgresses the borders of internal and external realities, both in children and adults.[20] The worlds of facts and imagination belong together in this potential space and are inseparably wedded to each other. The object in the mind symbolizes a reality derived from beyond the mind, but the symbol does not merely reproduce or accurately mirror that reality. The artist does not invent illustrations or other pictorial representations. The artist is perceiving reality in a distinctive manner, receiving a fresh disclosure from a beyond that knows and evokes depths within. The artist's work evokes a truth about objects and invites the viewer to a relation with objects that is not evident to noninvolved perception. Similarly, religious knowledge and self-knowledge are characterized by a quality of discovery: "Knowledge of ourselves, as of God, must in a sense wait until things are disclosed to us. The pace and scope of both proper self-knowledge and knowledge of God are not wholly under our own control."[21]

Referring to this quality of being not quite inside and not quite outside, Louis Weil can say, "All symbols are called to reveal and to remind, to join some physical element or historical event with what is perceived in faith as an articulation of the grace and presence of God. This joining, this symbolizing or throwing together of visible and invisible reality, lies at the heart of the Christian revelation."[22] In the life of Simone Weil this vision was presented with urgency: "We must feel the reality and presence of God through all external things, without exception, as clearly as our hand feels the substance of paper through the pen-holder and the nib."[23]

19. W. W. Meissner, *Psychoanalysis and Religious Experience* (New Haven, Conn.: Yale University Press, 1984), 183–84.

20. See Don W. Winnicott, *Playing and Reality* (London: Tavistock Publications, 1971), 1–25.

21. Frazer Watts and Mark Williams, *The Psychology of Religious Knowing* (Cambridge: Cambridge University Press, 1988), 98.

22. Louis Weil, "Worship and Pastoral Care," 115.

23. Simone Weil, *Waiting for God*, 13, 14.

One might think of it this way: As the temple in Jewish tradition and the church in Christianity are considered to be particular loci of the divine presence, so the human soul is the locus of God or the spiritual temple (1 Cor. 3:16), but the referent for that locus is transpsychological or transpersonal. Christian faith tells us that God is everywhere, that God transgresses the boundaries, is both internal and yet beyond. Likewise, one's mental images of God have a transitional quality, are received from beyond oneself and at the same time are deeply embedded in the heart. God is not reducible to one's images of God, yet there is a connection. Images have the potential to facilitate divine-human communication and communion. Accordingly, Christians think of humanity as made in God's image and likeness, and they believe that Jesus Christ is the true representation of the love of God.

But what from a psychological view is creation or construction is deconstruction from a sociological view. To enter into the creativity of transitional life and its transitional objects is to change position in relation to ordinary consciousness. As Victor Turner has analyzed in terms of ritual, a liminality is permitted and entered into.[24] Such liminality disregards ordinary assumptions and perhaps radically questions them. The contents of such liminality, the transitional objects and the world they inhabit, are extrinsic to the situations in which we find ourselves. Not only does life come to us with its familiar faces and its surprises, but also we come to the situations we face with an internal world, much of it unconscious. The internal habits of mind and heart are inside the person, but outside of— not intrinsic to—the situation in which the person stands. An external crisis may intrude into one's customary life. At the same time, one's internal world may intrude in a situation, as if it were an external factor intervening and bring new order or toppling it into chaos.

The potential space of psychic life, culture, and religion is the place where "objects" are not merely captured mentally for retention, but where possible relations with others are considered. Thus potential space is located between the past recapitulated in perception and memory and the future creatively entertained. Such creative thought produces new action or ways of relating to others, the world, and God. When the action or repositioning effectively expresses creative vision, the action has a symbolic quality— it communicates powerfully the new possibility to others and to self and invites and entices into this possibility. Accordingly, this sphere of potential space is the basis of meaningful action. Realistic vision recognizes that there are limits in a particular social situation, but the limits cannot be

24. Victor Turner, *The Ritual Process: Structure and Anti-Structure* (Chicago: Aldine, 1969).

predetermined—they can only be tested, and vision cannot resist testing the limits. After all, social situations, including belief systems, are distillations of imperfect apprehensions. J. B. Metz speaks of orientation toward the future, which here is located in potential space, as "passion for the possible."[25] Just as imagination has a social origination in the child's interaction with primary caring others, so mature imagination is characterized by a social dimension: It is imagining with others insofar as imagination is stimulated by others and is submitted to others.

To describe transitional space is to comment on the dynamics and wonder of the way in which experience of self and experience of other are inextricably tied together. From earliest mental life the child is motivated socially as well as biologically; that is, not only does the infant seek the fulfillment of instinctual demands, pleasures, or wishes, but he or she also seeks and takes pleasure in relating to the other, to the primary caring person, to the mother. The relationship to this other is a primary relationship, a relationship that exists for its own sake and is part and parcel of one's own self-concept. Children tend to trust their experiences of mysterious presence and their God-representations for these experiences. Adults come to suspect their own experiences and thinking, and they learn disciplines for self-correction. Unless they have become thoroughgoing skeptics, however, they affirm the value of their thinking and the significance of that to which it refers, including the reality of God, although that is far from perfectly apprehended. They take leaps of faith between one experience and another.

Clearly, then, psychological analysis cannot substitute for theology. Although humans' representations of God are rooted in human experience, and although it may be true that the divine relation will inevitably be interpreted primarily in terms of one's internal representation of God, still the reality of God is not the same as one's mental representation of God. W. W. Meissner puts the matter this way: "Thus it is not the God-representation which is loved; rather it is through the quality of the God-representation that the image of the God who is loved comes to express itself."[26] In simpler terms, Roy Fairchild is attributed to have defined praying as bringing all we know of ourselves to all of God that we know.

25. J. B. Metz, "Creative Hope," *Cross Currents* 17 (1967): 171–79.
26. W. W. Meissner, *Life and Faith: Psychological Perspectives on Religious Experience* (Washington, D. C.: Georgetown University Press, 1987), 52.

Chapter 2

Dialogue: The Entrance

I have discussed the fact that human beings have mental images of God and the concept that the reality of God is not reducible to such images. Further, I have argued that the foundational layer of the divine image is modeled on perceived relation to the primary caring other. Just as a significant part of one's creative capacity is born out of the early experience of being cared for and played with, so the childlike image of God derives from this experience. In a definite sense, preparation to pray begins with infancy, when children first begin learning to differentiate self and other, experiencing the presence and absence of the primary caring person in their lives, and constructing a mental representation of God and relating to this new presence in their lives. Because of this, "primary speech" is a helpful image for the phenomena of prayer.[1] In light of this coterminal inherence of the concepts of self and God, it is helpful to consider the definition of worship attributed to Carlyle Marney: "Our worship has to do with who God is, but it also has to do with who we are and who we wish to God we were."

Common Prayer

So, psychologically, to prepare to worship is to enter a transitional space, a place where the living image of God, the community and the individual self are closely bound together. Whatever the worshipers' personal, subjective frames of mind at the gathering, to begin to worship is to hark back to their foundational self-images as persons and as a people

1. Barry Ulanov and Anne Ulanov, *Primary Speech: A Psychology of Prayer* (Atlanta, Ga.: John Knox Press, 1982).

attended to by a God who is present. In a sense those at worship create this gap between the immediacy of subjective mood and the leap of faith. They believe that God is always present, although they do not always "experience" this presence. Yet, it is not entirely their own doing: They are led into this, just as an individual's self-image springs from depths that often transcend momentary feelings. They are drawn to worship; they are lured into the transitional place where symbols disclose their fragmented lives and make them whole again. They hear these words spoken to them and coming from their own mouths, and faith is born again.

Writing about the occasional rituals that mark life cycle transitions—such as baptism and marriage—Wesley Carr comments, "The ritual naming of a transition constitutes an object outside oneself with which, however, one is very bound up."[2] The same can be said of regular worship, because it marks the daily encounter with transitional experience. Worship is a ritual naming and enacting of the transitional experience called prayer.

When Christians pray, they are called to worship God together. Thus prayer is not allowed to be only a private reliving of a personal image of God, but becomes a dynamic encounter between internal images—those within the individual—and external images—those presented by a community as the fruit of its history and tradition. Public prayers recall a history and so make present a history to the psyche. Thus the spirit and its inner space are permeated by an outside world, a world that binds souls together in a common mentality and sensitivity. What faith remembers makes up the central "facts" of the soul, the objects of believing that are known by a historical "thereness" yet are not reducible to natural phenomena. The interaction of the internal and external enables the images to be truly symbolic, to point beyond themselves to the presence of the infinite. Private, internal images, when they remain private, do not effect change and do not undergo change. They step onto the threshold of change when they are juxtaposed with external objects that resonate with meaning, that is, external objects that come alive to the soul and have symbolic power. This threshold area contains an internal-external dialogue and flux. Such an area is like a border between two countries, a border people tend to take for granted except when they are crossing it.

Public prayer is united prayer, common prayer. It is prayer that takes worshipers out of themselves as separate from others and from God and so enables them to return to their deeper, essential selves. It is the prayer of worshipers' common humanity before God. Participation in the worship of a community of faith provides the individual with a system of checks

2. Wesley Carr, *Brief Encounters: Pastoral Ministry through the Occasional Offices* (London: SPCK, 1985), 26.

and balances in the individual psyche. What is private is confronted regularly with what the community is prepared to affirm and confirm. Also, participation in worship provides a secure, supportive environment. One is included as part of a community, is accepted and welcomed—despite all culpability and limitations—to a place where one can hope to encounter the holy. Psalm 52:8 sets forth this image: "I am like a green olive tree in the house of God." This tree, the human spirit, flourishes not in nature, outside, but in the house of God, a unique environment where the spirit is nurtured and grows to its full health and ripeness.

And so Christians pray as priests for one another: "The Lord be with you." Their speech becomes a doorway to the sacred. Although they may not regularly think of themselves as priests, here they act as priests, and in these symbolic acts become priests. Do not such actions express a belief, however subliminal? If they do, then the unusual language of the liturgy helps to reestablish emotional contact with aspects of its worshipers' self-images that they tend not to use consciously in their daily functioning and that challenge their ordinary self-understanding.

SUBJECT AS OBJECT

The "presence" and the "absence" of God are social metaphors, embedded experientially in people's earliest primary relationships. In worship persons bind themselves to one another within the framework of a shared image of God—not an image that can be reduced to that first childhood image, yet one that is related to its caring and spontaneous aspects. The shared understanding of God is an image that has developed and emerged as individuals have participated in family life, as people have worshiped together and helped each other catch the vision that has been creating them and is redeeming them and shall make them whole. Each worshiper's own self-understanding is framed in relation to that image of the Present One, yet all know that their symbolic language and mental images—although they bind them to this reality—do not fully contain or perfectly represent the divine mystery. They realize that their knowledge and its images are inadequate, yet they believe that the Attending One does know them ("Almighty God, to whom all hearts are open, all desires known, and from whom no secrets are hidden. . . ."), is present for their sakes, and even is present that they may come better to know the divine mystery insofar as this knowledge grows through love and adoration (". . . that we may perfectly love you, and worthily magnify your holy name . . ."). Deep down they recognize that the object of this contemplation actually is the subject. Mentally and emotionally they are encountering the wonder of knowing that they are being known by another beyond themselves who is present to and in them. It is a small step from this sense of divine presence to the conclusion that the worshipers are subjects only because they are "objects" in God's mind, that they have being because they are held in and by the loving gaze of God, that they love because they are loved. They aim toward being known so that they can know themselves in the context of living relationships between themselves, God, and others.

This leads to a paradox: How can God truly be Other and real as Other, and yet be a thought under the sway and control of a thinking subject? How can God be encountered as God? Images and thoughts of God are constructed in mental life, yet God is there, preexisting and waiting to be so created. Even though one's thoughts and beliefs are not sufficient to adequately represent God's reality, God permits and uses such processes in God's own mysterious way.

The human experience of personal presence is based on awareness of another person being there, attending to us, so the present experience of presence is an intuitive sense of being known, and the wonder of this knownness (knowledge that is from another position) offers a perspective not contained in familiar self-knowledge as fixed from past experience. Awareness of God's presence enhances this phenomenon because the sense of wonder is directed to the personal knower whose attending, knowing and loving are unimaginatively great.

Can it be inferred from this that one dimension of the dynamic of worship is that worshipers use a common language for God, yet grow in their understanding of God? Does this language in the context of worship, in a liminal and transitional "place," in spirit and in truth, in the openness of love and awe, evoke fresh images and insights? Does loving enrich or even transform worshipers' image and understanding of God? Is it possible, consequently, that participation in such ritual is like participation in a psychodrama that promises to correct and open up new possibilities for understanding God and oneself?[3]

RECAPITULATION

What, then, has been inaugurated by this initial psychological analysis of the beginnings of prayer in corporate worship? On the one hand, we are discovering that the workings of the liturgy and of nonliturgical prayer carry incalculable significance because they are bound up with worshipers' deep-seated sense of themselves; that a particular realm of creativity opens up these originating self-portraits and transforms them; that a time and place exist where different images of self and others are "played with," perhaps seriously as is the case with much play; that human beings swim

3. On the concept of ritual as participatory psychodrama, see Ruth Tiffany Barnhouse, "Secular and Religious Models of Care," in James E. Griffiss, ed., *Anglican Theology and Pastoral Care* (Wilton, Conn.: Morehouse-Barlow, 1985), 57–84.

out into this pool of personal and communal transition far more than they let themselves know consciously. In the beginnings of prayer persons already are transformed, if only for a time; they discover a new freedom, if only for a moment or two. Even if apparently transitory, such moments should not be discounted—they disclose a potential and manifest a powerful presence.

On the other hand, this psychological analysis gives very little. It has yielded only a different metaphor with which to reexamine prayer and the texts of public worship. It has yielded the notions of "potential space" and "transitional object," but their power to make us think derives in part from the fact that we do not know precisely what they designate or mean. Perhaps we cannot fully understand their meaning, but they do not reduce the reality of God to childish images. Rather, they testify—by their own creative incompleteness and by their power to suggest and not to answer—that human experiencing flows fundamentally out of a mysterious reality, a reality not reducible to the subjective or objective categories of humans' conscious habits of mind. Human sensory equipment for perceiving is organically intertwined into an imagining process so that there is no immaculate perception, only a creating response to stimuli, but one that is usually not under the control of intentional consciousness. Instead, such response is given. Creative artists do not make up an alternative version of what they perceive. Rather they "perceive" the vision that comes to them. The psyche is a bend in the stream of reality, a drop off whereby reality cascades to new life below the waterfall.

Although this analysis does not give much in the sense of resolving questions about prayer, it does put into question the suspicion that prayer is mere self-talk. The suspicion that prayer is a powerful means of self-suggestion has run up against the radical sociality of the self, so that being a self requires another. Furthermore, the "inner" thoughts of an individual constantly transgress the boundary that individuals posit between inner and outer realities; those inner thoughts operate in a social context and are designed to facilitate the life of social relationships, even if not all of these thoughts and mental images are very adequate. Further still, human thinking is so fundamentally symbolic and metaphorical that it is destined to open human beings to the never-ending presence of the Transcendent One who sustains and yet transforms without end. Consequently, prayer is more dialogue than self-talk.

Pastoral Care among People in Daily Life

The focus of attention has been on prayer, particularly prayer in public worship. Psychological reflections on such prayer have brought us to the place where we can begin to envision the significance of prayer as the soul of pastoral care. The analysis has retained the communal and social dimensions of prayer and disclosed how staunchly embedded in these is the personal dimension of prayer. The task now is to consider pastoral ministry beyond the sacred space of the sanctuary—that is, pastoral care among people in their daily life and work and in the midst of their personal and family crises.

BEGINNING TO PRAY

Prayer in the liturgy signals where all prayer begins—with the presence and absence of God, with the presence and absence of others, and with self-image. If all prayer begins here, so does prayer in pastoral care.

If the ministry of pastoral care and counseling is indeed one of a kind with the ministry of public worship, then one might consider that the pastoral act is a present rendition of a past prayer or prayers. It is as if a pastor's entire past were preparation for prayer in this moment of pastoral encounter, and as if a parishioner's entire past were preparation for prayer in this moment as well. Although prayerfulness and said prayers should not be isolated from each other, the former is more fundamental to pastoral care than the latter. This is why Kenneth Leech can write, "The ministry [of spiritual direction] is not so much a skill to be acquired as an overflow from a life of prayer and waiting on God."[4] Indeed, the same needs to be said of all ministry, including all of pastoral care and counseling.

Daily prayerfulness signals that the sluice between public worship and personal enactment of faith is open. Usually such prayerfulness requires disciplines beyond public worship. Actually, prayerfulness in public worship eludes many ministers at particular times in their careers because they become preoccupied with their leadership role and its demands. Sometimes it is only personal disciplines of prayer that revitalize public worship for ministers. If public worship sustains the soul of pastoral care, personal prayer is the first act of pastoral care: "It is on his knees that the pastor must first exercise his pastoral care."[5]

In any case, the rivers of public and personal prayer are destined to flow into the lake of prayerfulness so that more and more everyday life becomes a prayer offered to God. Then prayer is not only the words one says to God but also a way of being. Genuine and deep caring is the outcome of such prayerful living. In this way religious disciplines bless and infuse all of life with divine grace. They are a means to this kind of

4. Kenneth Leech, "Spiritual Direction and the Struggle for Justice," in Griffiss, *Anglican Theology*, 51.
5. Pius Parsch, *The Liturgy of the Mass*, 3d ed., trans. H. E. Winstone (London: B. Herder Book Co., 1957), 266.

end and not an end themselves in the sense of being a separate realm in which alone grace is to be found. Accordingly, Piet Fransen writes,

> Grace signifies rebirth in Christ. It denotes a mysterious but nonetheless eminently real stream of life which wells up from the deepest stratum of our being where it rests securely in the creative hand of God, up through all the slowly developing stages of our personality, irrigating and permeating the innumerable areas of our complex psychology, yet never ceasing to be a divine life, a purely gratuitous gift, God's constantly renewed and freely bestowed love.[6]

PRAYER AS RESPONSE TO GOD

Because prayer is the soul of pastoral care, prayerfulness is the key to meaningful and effective pastoral care. But does this say anything about specific prayers with those to whom one ministers? It is certainly possible to participate in worship by mindlessly voicing the prayers so that they are only the body of the liturgy; it is also possible to discover prayerfulness in a pastoral visit without the voicing of prayers. What is one to make of this?

In pastoral care ministry there are two extremes: Either one rushes into prayer or avoids it altogether. Prayerfulness helps pastors and counselors to avoid either extreme. The first guideline can be suggested by a series of questions: Is the prayer that counselors and ministers have with people a response to God? Is it a response to God's presence in this pastoral visit? Or is it a response to a memory of God's presence, a memory that presses itself on the present moment? (Note carefully that prayer is not just for the times when God's presence is felt—the experienced absence of God also cries out for prayer.) Is it a response to a genuine desire to pray (which is not the same as a request for prayer)? In short, the question for those engaged in a specific instance of pastoral ministy is this: Has God called them at this particular time to pray with this person or family? The first guideline thus becomes: Ministers and counselors are permitted to pray only when they already have. To hear the call to prayer is already to have begun to pray. Prayer as authentic response usually stands opposed to the conventional prayer at the end of a visit, to the pastor's ritual escape, and to the pastor's unthinking need to comply quickly with a request. Prayer as authentic response contrasts with prayer that triggers unconscious repetitions. Where there is pathos let there be prayer. The real problem is not deciding whether to offer prayer with or for a person. The real problem is praying a prayer that is received from God.

---

6. Piet Frans Fransen, *Divine Grace and Man,* trans. George Dupont (New York: Mentor-Omega Books, 1962), xiii, xiv.

PRAYER AS RESPONSE TO PEOPLE

The next question when considering prayer with others is this: Is the prayer a response to the person or persons to whom one is ministering? Faith affirms God's attentiveness, even though those with faith are not always conscious of God's presence. In light of that affirmation, it would seem that pastoral counselors and ministers are to be attentive, especially to others. Not that they possess God or can give God to others, but there may be times when their attentiveness is the occasion when others are reminded of God's caring presence. Can Christians listen to God without also listening to their brothers and sisters? And can they listen to their brothers and sisters without also listening to God? Perhaps it is shortsighted and unimaginative to think of listening as only empathy for another person.

Dietrich Bonhoeffer taught that we must learn to pray from Christ and not use "the false and confused speech of our hearts."[7] Certainly God leads Christians to prayer and shows them how to pray. But this prayer does not, I contend, require the repression or suppression of the speech of the heart. Rather, that speech, which well may be confused and even false, needs to be attended to and lifted to God, who alone can accept and transform it. Bonhoeffer is right that the Psalms are at once the word of God and a prayer to God. I ask: Is there no confused speech in the prayers of the Psalms? Even if the cultural, political, and judicial contexts of that time are considered, some psalms still sound paranoid. I suggest that God is being asked to hear human beings' own speech, even in its false consciousness and confusion. When this is done, the transformation that takes place in the people and the prayer itself is striking. When God enlightens them, they know how to let go of wrong desire, and their prayers and very selves are transformed.

Accordingly, I believe that pastoral prayer requires full attentiveness to the other. It is only when ministers and counselors love and care for others that they learn how to pray with and for them. Attending to others when conversing with them leads to a noticeable concreteness and even precision in prayers. At times, the conversation is such that the minister or counselor knows exactly how to pray, but when asked to offer prayer, usually it is better not to comply quickly; rather it is best to prepare to pray by engaging others in a discussion of what they desire to be lifted to God. This is far more difficult than creating one's own prayers, but often it leads to a new depth of communication with people, and that indeed makes genuine communication with God possible.

Such attentiveness discloses both the desire for and resistance to God. Prayer expresses a struggle between a readiness to honor God and an

---

7. Dietrich Bonhoeffer, *Psalms: The Prayer Book of the Bible* (Minneapolis: Augsburg Books, 1970), 11.

inclination to resist God. While pastoral counselors and ministers can recognize that the experience of absence communicates some aspect of God's reality, they do well to acknowledge and confess that often this absence reflects their own insularity in relation to God. Not always but many times psalms complaining of God's absence also are confessions of sin. As I recall, the Stoic Musonius Rufus had a sense of this when he asked: "What are you waiting for? . . . Until God in person shall come upon you? . . . Cut off the dead part of your soul and you will recognize the presence of God."

The second guideline for prayer thus becomes: Prayer is first a response to God, but it also involves a response to people—communicating openly with them and attending to them in a way that helps open them and their concerns to God.

THE DIALOGUE OF PRESENCE AND ABSENCE

Fundamental to pastoral ministry is the task of responding with deep care to personal experiences of the presence and absence of God. The presence and absence of God are not always thematized by parishioners, patients, or passersby who are under the care or seek the care of pastors, but these experiences are there and fuel the joys and agonies of living. Can they be discovered without prayer or without something very like prayer?

Prayer helps make available to persons their own image of God, self, and others; it opens them up to these images. Further, prayer can open them to listening (to others, to Christian tradition) at a level deeper than intellectual comprehension or objective consideration. Because this is so, I ask: Can pastoral care become genuine dialogue with others without prayer or something very like it?

People, whether "religious" or not, defend themselves against experiences of the presence and absence of God. Some of these experiences, after all, are associated with primitive images of God by and large put to rest long ago. The trouble is that a crisis can induce regression that makes such images available, although they may be unwanted. The mere presence of a religious professional may threaten to evoke these unwanted memories. Just as the pastor is a symbolic figure, a transitional object, for the people of God in public worship, so the pastor is a symbolic object in pastoral care. The common term for this phenomenon is *transference*. Very often the pastor's task is one of being there, allowing herself or himself to be used symbolically (which requires trust in the other person and trust in God), and providing a supportive yet free environment where the primordial can be encountered. Quite frequently the emotional and spiritual experience of the absence of God is a transition, a potential movement, from one image of God and self to another image of God and self. Such movement is an emotional and spiritual death and rebirth, and as such it requires a caring ministry of midwifery, a warm and steadying presence. Ministry at such times requires a rhythmic relating that is both an emotional "holding" or support and an undemanding presence or being there with persons, a presence that provides emotional space and freedom for them. Such ministry requires a living community and its human representatives. Can pastors be available in this way without prayerfulness?

Frequently personal support and availability are adequate to enable the emotional transition and spiritual adventure to take place. Just as often, however, the ministry of presence is not sufficient. The presence must take on the characteristics of a dialogue, one in which the old images of God and self are encountered by new ones. One must not forget that the transitional space of persons is not empty, not a tabula rasa. Yet in the realm of the transitional a dialogue is not a debate, at least not between the pastor and the other person. The pastor proffers, or gently suggests, images for the person's own reflection or inner debate.

An encounter with the primitive can be redemptive if these images are addressed by more adequate images of God. Individual fantasy, especially unconscious fantasy, does not transform itself. In ministry one person listens to another in a manner that evokes and at times proffers new images of God for the other's consideration. This is "inductive guidance" and there is a place for it, so long as it does not substitute for eductive guidance. One problem with inductive guidance is that the other person often is prepared only to be defensive regarding an image of God, and so it becomes impossible to discover truly meaningful and helpful alernative images. Inductive guidance at best does not offer simply another selection for the inclination of the moment, but helps to discover, or discovers and shares, the image of God that in the present hour grasps the soul with radical, unimagined love. How can one be prepared for such an endeavor without prayer and prayerfulness?

To speak of images of God and of experiences of the presence and absence of such images is to speak psychologically. Such discourse can refer to meanings but not to truth. Are some images closer to the truth and reality of the divine mystery than others? Does the transcendence of God obliterate all distinctions of true and false? Most religions set forth a cluster of understandings of the divine as most worthy of acceptance. In Christian faith, the true God is one of historical justice and grace, who was fully human and present in history, a God who readily forgives and who constantly calls to renewed right and full living. Out of such emphases many concrete images ring true and are productive at particular times and places. A pastor hopes to discern one emerging in the perspective of a parishioner, or to be able to proffer one that resonates with the heart of the parishioner. To use William James's phrase, certain visions are "living options"—they have plausibility in the soul. The gift of discernment is not the ability to peek into another's soul to decide what is good and bad therein. The gift of discernment sorts out what is happening in the interchange and exchange between persons in pastoral conversation and with God in prayer.

The inductive task is one of discovering images that celebrate, heal, sustain, guide, and reconcile in a particular situation. An image that does not speak to pastors is not likely to speak to parishioners. An image that may potentially be fresh for a parishioner but no longer is fresh for the pastor is likely to be communicated in a patronizing manner—even when one intends not to. So the challenge is to discover an image that is fresh and true—mutually so. Can this be done without prayer or something very like prayer?

PRAYER AND THE GOD OF SCRIPTURE

The dialogical quality of conversations, prayers, and prayerfulness in pastoral care leads to this question: Is the prayer a response to the God of Scripture? C. S. Lewis prayed, "May it be the real I who speaks. May it be the real Thou that I speak to."[8] Christians come to know this God by hearing Scripture and through the influence of lives that have been shaped by the God disclosed in Scripture. Of course in pastoral visits pastors hope that their manner of relating to others communicates their own understanding of a God who is attentive and gracious, who is lovingly there when people rejoice and when they suffer. Furthermore, pastors can share the prayers of Scripture with people, and do so in a respectful, nonimposing manner. In time of crises prayers can be dialogues between the God of Christian faith and individuals' limited construals of God that no longer enable them to cope. Such prayer is a co-orientation to self and God, and at the same time a reorientation to the God of Scripture and to the new self-understanding such reorientation makes possible. A time of crisis is likely to be a time when persons are more teachable. Exposure to and participation in the prayers of God's people can be the occasion of gracious transformation in self-understanding and knowledge of God. Pastors can invite others to join them in the Lord's Prayer. Many psalms can be prayed along with persons' prayers. And when these psalms are prayers, they should be addressed directly to God and not treated as Scripture readings. This juxtaposition accepts people's prayers and invites participation in prayer that clearly is addressed to the kind of God witnessed to in Scripture.

8. C. S. Lewis, *Letters to Malcolm: Chiefly on Prayer* (New York: Harcourt, Brace & World, 1964), 82.

The God of Scripture is present to the worshiping congregation and to individuals through liturgical prayers. Different pastors may have different emphases with respect to prescribed prayers and spontaneous prayers, but both have a vital place in pastoral care. Spontaneous prayers create free space for genuine self-expression on the part of pastor and people. Liturgical prayers provide boundaries for holding and supporting this space.

When pastors use the prayers of Scripture, they are more likely to realize that in their prayer they lift up both others and themselves. The mark of a significant pastoral visit is not a sense that the ordained minister provided a service to someone else. It is the recognition that in the course of that visit God has ministered to those present, pastor and lay. Because prayer creates a sense of togetherness, another mark of true prayer is the recognition of the presence of others, a larger community, the care of significant people in our lives, the presence of people of faith from all times and places. Prayer during pastoral visits binds persons to the worshiping community. Such prayers extend liturgical space beyond the sanctuary, the appointed place, connecting those who cannot attend public worship with the congregation and its living tradition. By using the organic metaphor of the church, Pius Parsch goes even further in expressing the connection between the corporate and personal dimensions of prayer: "Prayer is the breathing of the mystical body. Breath is an unmistakable sign of life. Consequently, where there is prayer, there the life of the Church is manifest, whether it is the prayer of the parish, the family, or individual souls, all of which are cells of the one Church."[9]

PRAYER AS THE FULCRUM OF CASE ANALYSIS

Protestant pastoral theology has acquired the habits of examining cases or various forms of reporting on life experience and of reflecting on theology in light of pastoral experience. My thesis leads me to suggest that the key focus of such reflection on cases should be on the "location" of prayer in pastoral ministry—its overt or covert presence, its overt or covert absence. To claim that prayer is the soul of pastoral care is not to promote piety as a panacea for the problems pastors encounter in their care of persons. As the depth dimension of pastoral care, Godward directed prayer is not something over which pastors assume complete control, but in their ministry they are accountable for their response to the calling of this depth dimension. Genuine prayer is not a strategy toward external ends in pastoral ministry. As the soul of pastoral care, prayer is a reality not to be taken for granted or paraded, as in much of pietism; nor is it a reality to which pastors should be total strangers.

9. Pius Parsch. *The Breviary Explained*, trans. William Nayden and Carl Hoegerl (London and St. Louis: B. Herder Book Co., 1952), 5.

Is prayer the fulcrum of case analysis? This is the question raised by my thesis. If so, a Clinical Pastoral Education supervisor could examine with a student chaplain and peers the text of a prayer voiced in the ministry event, or if none was voiced, as often is the case, examine a text of that student's prayer for the patient in light of the personal contact made. Likewise, whenever pastors reflect on their pastoral care with people, whether or not as part of a formal training program, they are likely to teach themselves best by using prayer as the fulcrum of analysis. In fact, the entire pastoral visit may be understood as a present rendering of a past prayer, as the offering and enactment of one's beliefs before God.

Pastoral care is a ministry of communication with God and people that draws its life from the community of prayer. Addressing this community Calvin said, "It is by prayer that we call him [God] to reveal himself as wholly present to us." Pastoral care is nothing if it is not a witness to the presence of God in all conditions of human life.

Even so, prayer discloses people's own poverty to them. The frustration of the one who prays is like that of the artist or any beholder of beauty— we want not merely to see beauty but to be united with it. But we cannot. The mystery transcends us. To ask about the limits of prayer is to ask about the limits of one's ministry. Indeed, can pastors claim to minister at all, especially when so often they receive more than they give in the course of their ministry? Pastors should remind themselves that Christ is the Pastor who makes some use of their assistance.

Limited as it is, pastoral ministry is a ministry of prayer, prayer from and with the One who prays for us. This ministry is not self-talk or manipulation. Rather it is communication, dialogue, with a genuine Other. This dialogue makes use of the images of the senses, transforming them into symbols as one makes what sense one can of the mystery of the divine presence. Prayer relies inevitably on the images of primary personal relations, and so one can interpret public and personal prayer as dialogue in the broad sense of both the words said and the communion and communication realized in silence. The conclusion here is not unlike that of Friedrich Heiler in his classic analysis: "Common prayer, therefore, insofar as it is a living thing of the mind, is really what in outward form it appears to be, a calling upon God, a speaking to God."[10] If one would know the soul of pastoral care, then one must become acquainted with prayerfulness, the prayers that are born out of prayerfulness, and the caring that grows from these.

---

10. Friedrich Heiler, *Prayer: A Study in the History and Psychology of Religion,* trans. and ed. Samuel McComb (London and New York: Oxford University Press, 1932), 336.

CHAPTER 3

Scripture: The Substance

"All scripture is inspired by God and is useful for teaching, for reproof, for correction, and for training in righteousness" (2 Tim. 3:16). Increasingly pastors (and caregivers) are discovering the value of meditating on Scripture and are beginning to explore ways to combine this approach to Scripture with the exegetical skills first acquired in seminary. Long nurtured in meditative practices, Roman Catholic clergy are now benefiting from a more vigorous emphasis on exegetical analysis of Scripture. These developments make for an informal convergence of the exposure these two groups have had to the Bible.

Meditative Aspects of Scripture

Here is the way a Protestant pastor describes his own experience:

I haven't set aside my seminary training with all the critical tools for exegesis, but I have become so enamored with the more meditative aspects of listening to Scripture that at moments I wonder if I'm still on solid ground—even though I feel that I am.

To be concrete, let me give you the gist briefly of my own reading of the story of Zechariah in Luke 1. As always I have acquainted myself with the textual and historical questions as well as the literary form and the larger context, but now there is a difference. Once upon a time (it seems that long ago!) I relied almost exclusively on the results of this study, straining for a gnat of meaning that I could serve up in a sermon with my integrity intact and in good, polished form. But now the intellectual data are a background that sets off a central truth: the parallel between Zechariah and me. Three years ago I had been depressed and angry about my pastoral situation. I got to a point in which I really believed that the congregation was not capable of doing any good or performing any effective ministry. I even had grave doubts about my personal ministry. I felt burned out, empty, and at the end of my rope. I seriously considered leaving the ministry. During that time I went through the motions of being a minister but without much spirit. Because of my serious doubting of accomplishing the mission God had given me in this pastoral appointment I did indeed become dumb as Zechariah. I opened my mouth to preach, but in reality nothing came out. This is hindsight, of course. At the time I was holding on to one thing as a stressed out minister: I saw myself as a good and responsible preacher. My pastor-parish relations committee let me know otherwise, and I was shocked to say the least.

Expecting that I might be pushed into some uncomfortable decisions, I began to pray. In fact, I started up again what I had not done in years: taking time for daily prayer and devotional reading of Scripture. It was two years ago that I initiated a systematic and disciplined time for daily devotionals in my life. What a great help that was for me. There were some wonderful moments when I truly felt thirst-quenching water pouring over me. By God's word through devotional use of Scripture and hymns I was blessed and in a sense born again, this time of the Spirit. I felt assured by God about my life, my personhood, and my call to ministry. I discovered ways to grow again as a husband and father. My old hunger for knowledge and ideas and facts has been overtaken by a deep-rooted hunger for God's word in my life. I realize now that in my preaching and teaching my sharing of Scripture was intended for the head and not for the heart. This left me with nothing real to say to others or myself. Just like Zechariah! I distinctly remember one church member telling me about a year ago, "I can understand what you are saying to us in your sermons." Other church members have been telling me of their being helped by my preaching. I know that my devotional use of Scripture is helping me in preaching God's word!

Perhaps it is just the ghosts of seminary professors in my mind, but I believe in what is happening in my life and ministry—I believe God has been doing this—and yet I do not believe—at times I wonder if I'm getting old and soft-headed. There is a chance that I am kidding myself, succumbing to subjective romanticism, and that when I see where it leads it will be too late. But the bond between me and the people is stronger and more vital—it's not imaginary! It's not like the consistency of popularity. I guess my real question has to do with how the objective skills of exegesis and the kind of personal appropriation of Scripture I have returned to are to be interwoven.

I cannot comment on the issues raised as one who teaches exegetical skills, but I do make use of these skills, and not for preaching alone. Much of my thoughts about pastoral care would never have come to the light of consciousness had I not been wrestling with scriptural texts in the detail that these skills demand. The pastor quoted above wonders how one is to balance objective knowledge and subjective meaning, the discipline of truth-telling and the freedom of belief. Experiences such as his bring to mind thoughts and questions from a pastoral care perspective. They relate both to questions of exegeting and praying the Scriptures and to the place of these as means of grace in the practice of pastoral care. The purpose of this chapter, then, is to examine the processes of studying the Scriptures and praying the Scriptures in the context of pastoral ministry.

A TUTORED IMAGINATION

If prayer is the soul of pastoral care, Scripture is the substance of pastoral care. Scripture is the well from which Christians draw the life of truthful caring. In the context of Christian faith, prayerful understanding of Scripture is the basis for true and truthful caring. Such listening to Scripture is multifaceted: It is corporate in the context of worship; it is to be a part of daily common prayer and personal devotions; it is exegetical, a critical and systematic mode of listening; it is dialogical in the context of Christian ministry (what early Christians and Calvin termed "fraternal correction"); it is a patient and passionate waiting that is pregnant with new being and new action; it is a self-decentering and so self-liberating loyalty to the text that has authority to bring forth the authentic self in the process of encountering community in the cross fire of caring and truth-finding. To apply here the felicitous image used by Paul Pruyser, Scripture "tutors the imagination."[1] That is, it is the soulful, prayerful, yet intelligent hearing of the word of God that tutors the imagination. Intelligent and soulful attending of the word of God acquaints pastors and persons in their care with the One who is the way, the truth, and the life (John 14:6), whose footsteps one hears in the wilderness of the human situation, whose step and sound and voice one comes to trust (John 10:4).

The sense of playful proportion and careful craftsmanship called for in this multifaceted listening is hinted at in something Peter Gomes once said in conversation: The basic obstacle to biblical preaching is that preachers trust neither the text nor themselves. And so I raise this question: What kind of work and what kind of nonwork (pure attending) escort pastors to the one place where they do trust both the text and themselves? Also, I wonder if the trail to this place is not made muddy when the goal envisioned is the preaching of a sermon on the text. Such a goal is inevitable—for after all, ministers are preachers. And such a goal is worthy—a good sermon is certainly hard to find. Yet, the goal as such needs to be challenged,

1. Paul W. Pruyser, "The Tutored Imagination in Religion," in Paul W. Pruyser, ed., *The Changing Views of the Human Condition* (Macon, Ga.: Mercer University Press, 1987), 101–15.

for proclamation has many forms both in the ministry of pastors and in the ministry of all God's people. Although the many forms of listening may help to shape a sermon, not all listening is to be herded and corralled into the sermonic moment. And one dare not forget that the pastor teaches and preaches not just because he or she has had seminary training and so has the equipment and skill for interpretation. Just as significantly, the pastor teaches and preaches because he or she listens to the people listening to the Word of God.

The above-quoted pastor's own experience is suggestive. In his crisis he began to listen to the Word for himself as well as for others, and to listen to it at a deeper level. This change affected his personal relations as well as his preaching, and, no doubt, it affected his relationships with the people he served.

DIVINE READING

The concept of combining exegesis and prayer is hardly new. In commenting on Exodus 12:4, for example, Origen wrote, "Whence it is shown that we must not only employ zeal to learn the sacred literature, but we must also pray to the Lord and entreat 'day and night' that the lamb 'of the tribe of Juda' may come and himself taking 'the sealed book' may deign to open it."[2] Origin, by the way, is an interesting study in the relation of preaching and prayer. He included prayers within his sermons; he understood prayer to be the prelude and response to hearing the Word; and he believed that the prayers of the people make sermons effective.

To trust the text is to refuse to open it for oneself; to trust the text is to wait and let it be opened. There used to be a definite way of doing this. It was called *lectio divina*, or divine reading. In the strict sense the process was envisioned as having four dimensions: (1) *lectio*, reading and listening to the text; (2) *meditatio*, reflecting on the Word; (3) *oratio*, praying for the Word to touch the heart; and (4) *contemplatio*, encountering the silence too deep for words.[3] In the post-Enlightenment age the study aspects of this process have become more complicated and technical, and have come to dominate the way experts attempt to understand a text. The traditional scheme of *lectio divina* serves to remind Christians that what the Scriptures say is important and that what God does to them through the Scriptures is equally vital. Such is the way that leads to a text being opened for and to a person. Broadly speaking, *lectio divina* entails prayerful study and a

2. Origin, *Homilies on Genesis and Exodus,* trans. Ronald E. Heine, The Fathers of the Church 71 (Washington, D.C.: The Catholic University of America Press, 1982), 372.
3. Thelma Hall, *Too Deep for Words: Recovering Lectio Divina* (New York: Paulist Press, 1988), 36–56.

studied prayerfulness. Prayer precedes and follows exegesis, and prayer-fulness sits close by throughout the exegetical process. Because the term *lectio divina* points to a spiritual task and several dimensions integral to it, but as such is not a technique, I shall use the term broadly to refer to prayerful study of Scripture.

The concept of divine illumination alluded to above implies that what-ever analytical tools one employs, the fundamental task entails prayer or some kind of prayerfulness. As Timaeus said, "All men, Socrates, who have any degree of right feeling, at the beginning of every enterprise, whether small or great, always call upon God." The enterprise of exegesis is no exception. The reason some exegesis fails to disclose is not because it is technical or difficult but because it is undertaken with the presumption that exegetes are the ones who unlock the mysteries.

This is why I like the Reformed tradition's habit of a prayer for illu-mination before the reading of Scripture in corporate worship. In the Christian tradition to pray for illumination means essentially to trust in Jesus as the one who makes known the text. So trusting the text enough to wrestle with it intellectually, enough to brood over it, enough to stay with it, fighting but respecting its stubborn silence—this is possible only in the prayerfulness that looks to Christ, who is greater than we and who must increase as our pride and control decrease.

Psychological Aspects of the Word

The image of Christ is a fascinating representation in the mind, for simultaneously and always Christ represents humanity and God. The Christ alive and present "inside" the soul is indefinable except by reference to the "outside"—that is, to the historical Jesus, however elusive, and to the unfathomed, transcendent reality of God. To trust Christ is precisely to trust the Other and oneself. How can one locate the initiative to which trust is the response as being either within or beyond the soul? The locus precedes, permeates, and transcends inner and outer realities. Consequently, these inner and outer realms dynamically inhere. Knowing Christ, then, is more than a conscious representation in the mind of a historical story and character; it is a reshaping, a being conformed to, and becoming like that which one knows (Eph. 4:13). This knowing is the core of personal development or formation, and is the seedbed of action, personal and corporate. The inherent relation of knowing, being, and action, such that true knowing forecasts destiny in terms of identity and action, will be developed at a later point.

Earlier, I asserted that the divine process of self-revelation is analogous to the natural process of the formation of the self in relation to the primary caring other. God's self-giving is like the mother's self-giving, and as the mother mirrors the child, occasioning the child's self-discovery, so God mirrors to people their true nature in Jesus Christ. In Christ persons come to understand the nature of God and their own identity. Accordingly, praying the Scriptures is listening to Christ as the one who interprets the Scriptures (Matt. 9:7; Luke 9:35; 24:27).

But if from an experiential standpoint Christ is a transitional reality, transcending internal and external boundaries of self and other, so is Scripture. Existentially, all people have personal "canons," texts that tell them who they are, texts to which they listen in a particular way because these texts strike the heart. The Bible is the canon set before Christians who are called to listen to its texts in order to uncover false self and discover true self. This false self occupies the center of its own world; it is egocentric; it deploys battalions of assumptions, programmed emotional reactions, and mental and behavioral habits that occupy much of the territory of daily life.

Dynamically, everyone's personal canon is mixed, and that is the problem. Human beings have not yet attained one mind or what Kierkegaard spoke of as purity, the capacity to will one thing. The psychological "canon" is a conglomeration of inner "texts," which are primary sources for self-understanding and together set the boundaries or limits for this self-understanding. Where there are no boundaries, there is no knowledge, only chaotic mental process, but misplaced boundaries distort true knowledge. Christians see Christ as the image of the invisible God (Col. 1:15), as the one through whom God executes right judgment (Acts 17:29-31), and as the truth-discovering way and limit on the endlessness of human imagings. Pride and other forms of sinfulness misdirect the imagination (Luke 1:51), which is in need of continual redirection.

The Scripture is what Christ, our tutor, sets before us to train the imagination (Luke 24:27), and so the Bible itself occupies a place in the psyche and represents the voice and spirit of Christ. The point is that, inspired as is the content of the Bible, its status of authority as canon introduces a dynamic that enters into the reading and analyzing of any part of it. Think, for a moment, of how corporate worship begins—typically with sentences of Scripture. This way of beginning authenticates the voice of the leader as representing the word of God and the voice of the people. Whether the initial sentences are prayers or not, whether or not they refer to prayer, the sentences are calling the people to prayer. When the people hear Scriptures read and hear the accompanying words, they have the mental image of a primary Other who is speaking among them and within them. They are sheep who know this voice (John 10:4), and they enter into the potential space of that Other's spirit, or what can be called "liturgical space."

In passing, let me note that there is a definite analogy between texts and the primary mental representations discussed earlier. Like texts that do not change, these primordial images are relatively stable or "fixed" in the psyche, but their contexts and meanings can and do change over time, just as texts have a capacity for new meaning. For Christians the Bible is both canonical text and primordial object. This is why there is a perennial danger in this inevitable locus of the people's canon. Emotionally as well as spiritually, the Bible occupies such a special place that it readily is idolized. Some Christians worship the Bible and crazily forget the author. How can one tell when this is happening? This occurs when the Bible no longer says anything new to a person or community—it is sealed. This means that these people find themselves cut off, on the outside. Then they automatically and unconsciously project their needs onto the Bible, and what they receive back is nothing but their old, untransformed selves. Dynamically the meaning of Scripture is not only what it says but also what God does to people through Scripture.

So exegeting and praying the Scriptures are a means of grace, and like all such means are to be used as a way of actively serving God, but Christians' trust is in God, and confidence in the means of grace is relative to the giver of this hope and confidence. Christians' trust is in Christ, and so in God's Spirit of truth (John 16:13). Further, it is in Christ that Christians are made new creatures (2 Cor. 5:17). The Scriptures teach about this Christ, and he gives his followers understanding of them (Luke 24:27), so that they become a means of grace. As Howard Stone writes, "Faith involves the assurance that God's word *will* come, but not the knowledge of when or how."[4]

SCRIPTURE IN COMMUNITY

In gifting human beings with faith, God trusts them both as individuals and as a community. The Christian canon tells persons who they are, and it gives identity to the Christian community. In this community Christians share beliefs and enter into dialogue around the texts of their canon. Thus they enlighten and correct one another, so that the meanings delivered to them through the texts are not subsequently buried in individualistic isolation. When Christians listen to one another listening to the word spoken in the texts, then one can stand and speak a representative word, a word that represents what has been heard. Consequently, in corporate worship

    4. Howard Stone, *The Word of God and Pastoral Care* (Nashville: Abingdon, 1988), 71.

preaching may become a resounding and enlarging of the truth of Christ already present and speaking. This means simply that every congregation does well to have some definite means of studying Scripture, such as small groups for studying and praying the texts.

Christians come to trust the texts, then, in part because God has given them each other. They are called to care enough to listen and to speak the truth to one another. As they become open books to one another, the Bible becomes an open book, speaking to them in their daily lives: Christ is present among them. This is the way truth lives, in the midst. There is no immaculate perception, no perfect or complete possession of truth. The truth Christians discover will not be flattering, but it does provide definite hope and guidance for facing the future. The tools of exegesis are one corrective for the violation of the text by imposing self-illusions onto it; another corrective is the loving but honest dialogue among people committed to Christ, and consequently also to the Bible as the substantive and dynamic guide to Christ.

The Christian Scriptures have a distinctive place in the Christian tradition of this process of reorientation. This process decenters the old self, disclosing its fragmentation, and recenters life on God in Christ, present now in the Spirit. Because this process entails a deconstruction of ego-centered living, it is threatening and will be resisted with great vigor, although often unconsciously. This dethroning of the self usually occurs through the media of crises and tragedies, on the one hand, and peak experiences, on the other. It also occurs through the daily learning of the art of attending to Scripture, a developing capacity for mindfulness and fresh awareness. In any of these very different avenues, the person becomes aware of vulnerability, and the loving care of others is vital for support and hope. The word of Christ crosses swords with ordinary sense; it jars one out of the seat of self-control, and so is hard to hear (John 6:60). But the decentered, vulnerable self no longer constitutes itself, and so ceases, if only momentarily, to construct itself. Rather, one is so struck down in affliction or in honesty that he or she is hardly recognizable as a person or self, and is held by God, and can only trust God as a child trusts the caring strength of a parent who holds the child.

Lovingly prayed over, attended to, and combed through, the Bible becomes a living canon, the text that opens God to Christians and so opens Christians to themselves. As surely as one has a self-image (or has an internal representation of the self), one is a text to oneself. As Rupert Brooke wrote, "All things are written in the mind" ("Lines for an Ode— Threnody on England"). To refer back to Anton Boisen's metaphor, people are "living human documents," and they learn to interpret much of the meaningfulness of their lives in the light that comes from the Bible. Their own texts, their lives, speak to them because they are spoken to by Scriptures. This is why the meaning of *lectio divina* can be extended to include pastoral case studies, but a case study is likely to be pastorally and personally transformative only insofar as one loves and seeks to know the Bible and becomes more and more steeped in the Scriptures.

The dynamics of personal and cultural canons, primary texts that sustain selves and communities, disclose the emotional significance and spiritual centrality of the Bible as the substance of pastoral care. In order to sustain true care for people and for themselves, pastors must pray and exegete the Bible; they must attend to past and present theological interpretations of its meanings; they must seek dialogue between the primary sources of Christian faith and their contemporary experiences.

DIVERSITY WITHIN AND WITHOUT

In addition to the problem of a "mixed canon" within, the external, Christian canon (the Bible) is so diverse that it hardly seems to be of one mind. Is this diversity necessary to address the multiple contradictions of the human condition? Without multiplicity, no self can exist; without multiplicity, no canon is capable of negotiating a community and a self, of being a means of grace whereby humans become who they are meant to be in God's dream for them. Without paradoxical differences and unsettling strangeness, Scripture could not be "the pure and perennial source of the spiritual life" (Vatican II "Dogmatic Constitution on Divine Revelation," VI.21). From an experiential viewpoint, the Bible is worthy of canonical attention because it opens up and expands self-awareness; it discloses new possibilities for the self without denying the messy actualities of the self. In fact, under the tutelage of Scripture, the needier the self, the greater the possibilities. The prophetic word concerning Christ is a lamp in the dark recesses of human existence until "the morning star rises" in the human heart (2 Pet. 1:19).

The Pastor's Role

In pastoral care, then, does the pastor, by virtue of educational background and the personal discipline of listening for the word, tutor the parishioner's imagination? In a conventional way the answer is yes, yet fundamentally the answer is no. Christ, of course, is the teacher or tutor— Christ within the person or in the midst of persons, acknowledged or not. At best, the pastor assists the person in listening and attending to God's speaking in a particular situation, but this assisting is only a conventional posture in a situation in which both are listening for the word of God. Usually, at least in crises and transitional periods, the persons to whom a pastor would minister are more open psychologically than is the pastor. This is because a crisis or turning point has positioned them so that they are more teachable or at least capable of greater learning. This is why Anton Boisen focused on human crises. The drama in which God's presence and speech are disclosed is occurring in the life of the parishioner, and hopefully also in the interaction between parishioner and pastor. A crisis is like a spotlight that draws attention to a previously unlit part of a person's soul. More often than not, the pastor participates in a drama as a peripheral character and witnesses the wonder of the divine presence and speaking, and in this way becomes more open to the fresh, transforming message of God. The principal actor, as it were, is the parishioner, and to characterize the pastor as a tutor gives her or him too central and ego-satisfying a role, although there is an element of tutoring in a pastor's care of persons.

The pastoral role can be further elucidated by comparing it to the role of a psychiatrist doing psychotherapy. A patient relays the story of an illness. The physician takes this narrative along with a variety of observations and makes a diagnosis. The language of this professional diagnosis is not that of the patient, so typically the sufferer has one interpretation, and the professional practitioner has another. The healing process in part becomes one of negotiating or of dialogue or even of collaboration between these persons in the context of caring with the hope of healing. The pastor may not employ a language as technical as that of the psychiatrist, but the pastor does have a vocabulary, some of it religious, and a way of interpreting what he or she hears. The person who seeks pastoral guidance may also have a religious vocabulary, but may apply it in a different manner and direction than the pastor. The interpretative negotiation and dialogue between these perspectives, not all of it verbal by any means, take place in the context of caring with the hope of healing. So far it seems that the main differences between the practice of the psychiatrist and the ministry of the pastor are in the level of professionalization of the interpretative language and in the content differences in their respective languages. One might add that the psychiatrist symbolizes some form of authority to the patient, and the pastor symbolizes God and official religion. The psychiatrist ought constantly to relate his or her language and interpretation to the patient's language and to observations of the patient's experience and behavior, and might in this fashion help the patient to discover in the illness itself a source of wisdom. In this sense the physician is "an empathic witness," to use Arthur Kleinman's phrase.[5] Likewise, the pastor listens and learns and out of preparatory acquaintance with Christian sources may

5. Arthur Kleinman, *The Illness Narratives: Suffering, Healing, and the Human Condition* (New York: Basic Books, 1988).

discern Christ in the person or may be in a position to empathetically witness to Christ in relation to the person's suffering and self-understanding. If empathy is a moral act and attending to another a spiritual offering, then at a nonverbal level the word of God's loving and merciful care is being communicated already. And if this is so, then there is no need to arbitrarily or compulsively impose verbal interpretations or scriptural passages where these interfere with the dynamics of personal caring. It should not be forgotten, however, that verbal communication, not only of one's own care but also of God's, at times is a natural part of such caring.

SCRIPTURE AND PASTORAL CONVERSATIONS

Consider, then, what hopefully takes place in a pastoral conversation. Two or more persons whose lives are thrown together discover meaning as their relationship is transformed from polite introduction or tentative trials at real communication into a bonding together, an attentiveness to something sacred in and between them, a mutual affirmation and a mutual listening to what and who may be directing this affirmation. A pastor's process of understanding Scripture shapes his or her interpretation of this encounter of two or more lives, and other "texts" in his or her life that operate dynamically like a canon (for example, messages from childhood) also influence this interpretation. The others too have their personal "canons," and these guide what they hear and understand. But in these conversations, at least for the pastor, the canon to which loyalty intentionally is pledged is the Scriptures, which are concrete and overt and which carry the authority to tutor the imagination that will submit or agree to their transcendence—that is, the imagination that does not reify or make an idol of its own products. This does not mean that the pastor throws the Bible at people or lines up some proof text beside every issue or opinion. This would be to manipulate the canon, and a true canon operates on a different level: It creates action and understanding and is not a weapon for giving any one person authority over another. Rather, understanding of the Bible sensitizes pastors, teaches them what to look for in others and themselves, and prepares them to attend to God's presence, even in the least likely nooks and crannies of people's lives.

Yes, the Bible can and often should be read in the course of pastoral conversations. Howard Stone comments that the purpose of verbally communicating the Word of God in pastoral care "is not to manipulate or pressure the other person but to share something of personal importance to ourselves with this other person for whom we care so deeply."[6]

6. Stone, *The Word of God*, 75.

GUIDANCE FOR DIVINE READING

If parishioners in crises or in the ordinary course of Christian community are asking for guidance on divine reading or something like it, the pastor can teach straightforward methods such as the approach of Francis de Sales.[7] Usually persons try a method and go beyond it, readily adapting their own style of listening to Scriptures. All church libraries should have good commentaries for consultation, and the same is true for hospital chaplaincy departments, which ought also to consider a loaning library for patients and staff.

One person I know describes her discipline of reading Scripture as follows: "The first task is to empty my mind of surrounding concerns [in a sense to dislocate oneself]; then I replace my 'mind' and its ego-centered concerns with the text. The next step is to add the world so that it is the text and the world. Finally, I reintroduce my own reality and reflect on the text in relation to it." The strategy of this detour is to let the text speak and not simply use the text as a pretext for self-talk.

What happens when persons study and pray the Scriptures, and talk over their responses with others, perhaps the pastor? They are using texts of Scripture to compose their own "text"—to spell out their own understanding of God, their relation to God, and what God is saying now to them. Perhaps it is better to say that they are appropriating the text than to claim that they are constructing its meaning. At any rate, something in a text, for example, triggers a deeply held way of understanding or triggers an issue, perhaps cavernous and subliminal. The Scriptures, then, are relevant when they thus quicken the soul, or address the spirit of a community.

But do they merely "trigger" and all of the remainder is people's own process and construction? Emphasis may be placed on one or the other pole in this dialectic, but both are essential to an understanding of the human knowing and transitional space explored in meditation. Humanists, for example, tend to emphasize the human activity of construction, and the extreme view is the creation of meaning out of nothing (Sartre). At the other extreme is the emphasis on revelation, with the human subject receiving the truth without distortion. The experiential reality of divine reading negotiates its way between these ideal types.

The Scriptures are relevant and authoritative when they make us authors of a new community and a new self. The question is: What is the relation between the old self-understanding, the scriptural text, and the new self-understanding? Is the process one of being led, a process that may begin

7. Francis de Sales, *Introduction to the Devout Life* (New York: Harper and Row, 1966), 69–75.

where the old self is, yet moves on in such a way that the old self's limited perceptions and perspectives are decentered and even set aside? When a scriptural passage truly speaks and is genuinely heard, the encounter is vastly different and even strange when compared to the familiar process whereby the reading of a text merely occasions the rehearsal of old needs and established habits of mind.

Pastors do well to be attuned to these dynamics and to realize that in undertaking divine reading persons are venturing toward new discoveries of the reality of God and their relation to God and thus to others and to their own selves. Transitional space is a dynamic place. It may be the place of renewal and integration, or it may be the scene of annihilation. In fact it is both, for there is no new life without death.

What kind of new self is being formed when one listens to a text? Is the response to the text at least the initial stage of performing the text in one's own life or in a community's witness? As an interpretative performance, such a response is subject to self-reflection and criticism from and with others. The "potential space" in which this hearing and responding occur is at least personal and social. Yet it is somehow more. When creative, the process cannot be explained by discrete personal and social factors. The old cannot make sense of the new, but the new can give meaning to the old. Can one encounter the exhaustless newness of God and deny the reality of transcendence?

When Christians reflect on exegeting and praying the Scriptures, they see that the Scriptures have opened to them the reality of God as the agent in their lives. This is illustrated in the pastor's personal reflections quoted at the beginning of this chapter. The Scriptures opened the presence of God to him and the Spirit in turn opened the Scriptures to him. No doubt exegesis helped him to become more attentive to what is in the Scriptures, including the Lukan passage on which he focused, and precluded an arbitrary composing of his own text without really listening and without really being discovered by the text.

When one asks what kind of difference scriptural texts have made, can one identify how the newly launched self-understanding is both faithful and creative with respect to the Scriptures? Pastors need not be quick to voice their answers to this question for others. The greatest need is to be attentive. As persons relate their insights to pastors, often those persons begin to ask these questions for themselves.

A special moment in ministry occurs when a pastor has the kind of relationship with a parishioner that permits them to join together in silent meditation on a text, after which they mutually share insights and questions with each other.

Many persons, however, have had no discipline of listening to Scriptures and do not see the point of launching on such a project in the midst of a crisis. But does this mean that such persons are not in their own way listening for what God might be saying or wondering where God is in relation to what they are facing? Is it not possible for the pastor to be so attentive to them that these persons discover themselves listening to their own, hidden canons, their self-defining texts or mental images, in a manner that enables them to begin to author a new self-understanding and, at least implicitly, a new understanding of God? When the secret canons of one's soul are exposed to the light of consciousness, the first step has been made toward liberation from false self. Another step is encounter of the whole person with the word of God, which helps that person envision not only the false self but also the freedom *to* which God calls him or her. A liberating, new consciousness is evidence of the Spirit of Christ already within, a sign of the process of transformation. A pastor's listening helps to catalyze this process and positions the pastor to witness this process. And is it not possible, as mentioned above, for the pastor to share an insight from the Christian Bible, proffering it in a respectful, tentative, and timely way for that person's consideration, just as friends share perspectives with each other?

But I fear that readers will agree too quickly, especially to the last question. Agreement here is dangerous because it slyly invites pastors to step back into the pulpit while doing pastoral care, or to re-vision the pastoral conversation as a classroom. In pastoral conversations a little of the didactic goes a long way, and too much of it derails pastoral care. Pastors teach best by listening and learning. This is because, as St. Augustine knew, Christ is the teacher within and Christians simply help one another to remember and attend to his illumination in their souls.

With respect to the Scriptures, the paradigm for all of these phenomena in pastoral ministry is the study and praying of the Psalms. In liturgical traditions psalms are read or sung with each worship service, Sundays and daily. In pastoral care ministry, the Psalms are probably read more than any other portion of the Bible. Probably, when people in crises turn to the Bible, they turn most often to the Psalms for their own meditation and prayer. This is because, as Athanasius and so many others have understood all along, the Psalms address all conditions of life, thought, and spirit.

PASTOR AS SYMBOLIC OBJECT

The one who "presides" or leads is one who ushers worshipers into the sacred realm. This person inaugurates worship invariably with a sentence from Scripture. The saying has authority, and the speaker derives authority in part from this fact in order to call the community to prayer.

Psychologically, this one serves as a transitional object for the others. His or her bodily presence and role stimulate internal associations concerning God and the sacred. As the psychotherapist lets himself or herself be used as a symbolic object in a therapeutic relationship that reconstructs and reworks primary relationships, so the ritual leader becomes a representing "object," and a process of strengthening and correcting, of reconstructing, of fashioning and refashioning God-understanding and self-understanding commences.

The ritual leader in the life of the faith community is also the leader in the community's care of individuals. A complex, multidimensional symbolism adheres to the person and office of the pastor. This theme has been analyzed psychologically, but not adequately so, in terms of transference and countertransference. The faith community's ritual and pastoral leader becomes a symbolic object, a phenomenon pastors may experience as being abused or adored by a minority of parishioners at either extreme of a continuum.

I have claimed that, from a psychological viewpoint, persons have a personal "canon" that is essential to their self-definition. Such a canon is transitional in that it has outward forms and inner representations in dynamic tension. This personal canon functions as a transitional object or a set of such objects in the psyche. Likewise, the pastor in relation to the parishioner very well may serve as a transitional object, especially at a time of crisis or change. For this reason, although it is too much to claim that pastors are tutors, there is another sense in which the pastor's role is not so peripheral or on the sidelines. The fascinating thing is that the pastor may be more symbol than person in a relationship, although almost always there is a dialectic between the pastor as person (external) and the pastor as symbol in the internal life of another.

Pastoral availability is not just "being there," but is being present and willing to be such an "object." Because pastors are symbols, they often feel that they have done nothing for persons, yet these persons credit pastors with miracles. For the same reason, pastors often feel maligned and misrepresented and do not recognize themselves in others' portrayals of them. They may be seen as angelic or perfect; or they may be seen as the Antichrist. This is in part because some parishioners see pastors as embodiments of the Bible, and they drape their created image of faith over their pastors.

As a pastor, one's task is not to interpret the dynamics of transference or countertransference; rather, one's task is to be willing to be the symbol to help carry forward the conflict centered in the symbol. What does this mean? It means to be subject to misrepresentation and yet to be oneself, to decline to defend oneself and yet to offer oneself anew to God and to the other, no more and no less, as consistently as possible. In part, being oneself means not seeing others as they see themselves when they are "misrepresenting" one as a symbol. Each person who has a mental image of the pastor as a parental figure, an authority figure, or a representative of the divine has also a correlative self-image. If pastors get the message of how they are interpreted by their parishioners, they also have received indirectly the message of how the parishioners see themselves. It may be that people discern in pastors features that pastors refuse to recognize in themselves, and pastors have to consider that possibility. But in the event of distorted apperception of who they are, pastors can respond by being themselves, refusing to conform to the image projected onto them, and countering others' self-images by relating to them out of fresh vision of their possibilities. For pastors, to be themselves in such situations certainly does not mean retaliating because they feel abused. For pastors, being a true symbol even when others are inclined to misinterpret the symbol means being faithful to the pastoral office and its duties, which point to the truth of Christ. By being themselves, pastors behave in a fashion that is like the text that is stable and refuses to change and be anything other than what it is. Such behavior expects persons to come to the place where they see clearly what their pastor is, and a pastor's hope is that they will discern even there, in the pastor, some of the inexpressible love of Christ for them.

It is also the case, naturally, that pastors project their conflicts onto parishioners. They see ghosts and angels in parishioners. Their task is to attend to them as real persons, knowing them as if for the first time, and then what their lives symbolize will have new meaning.

This simultaneous offering of oneself as real object and as actual person, as bigger-than-life symbol and as concrete personality, is the kind of saintliness that is the order of the day in pastoral care and counseling. What is required for all this except the grace of attentiveness to Scriptures and to people, including one's own self? So it is that to be a pastor requires prayerful study and a studied prayerfulness. As Hebrews 2:1 suggests, either one attends to the word of salvation or one drifts.

Classical texts constitute a culture. Primordial texts constitute the self, giving self an identity. Between one's deepest self-image and one's most profound image of God lies a cluster of texts or a personal canon. Such texts fill the space of the human spirit, the potential space bounded by self, other, and the symbols or transitional objects that represent self/other relations. Scripture presents Christ to the liturgical life of the community and the imaginative life of the person, and so enables persons to listen more attentively to the Christ within. This Christ tutors the imagination so that persons can negotiate their way through the diverse promises and demands that would claim the spirit's allegiance. Because of its critical role in the faithful presentation of Christ, Scripture may be said to be the substance of pastoral care as truthful and enlightening care. When one attends to Scripture, Scripture renders a present agent (God), a new self, and a promising world.

Guidance is a vital aspect of the cure of souls. Pastors are called to help persons to attend to the enlightening Christ who is present with them. This call is strengthened and enhanced as pastors themselves learn to attend more freely and sensitively to the Christ presented in Scripture and present with them immediately in the Spirit and in the lives of others. Divine reading, praying and exegeting the Scriptures, is as essential to daily pastoral care as to sermon preparation. Along the paths of Scripture texts one learns to walk in the presence of Christ and to listen for the Christ speaking in the hearts of others as well as in one's own heart.

Chapter 4

Reconciliation: The Evangelical Principle

To begin considering reconciliation, pastors might recall the last time that they pronounced the absolution of sins to an individual or family who reviewed and confessed their faults. Many pastors assume that listening counts the most and that their personal acceptance of persons serves as the equivalent of a declaration of God's forgiveness. Some pastors consider most guilt feelings to be neurotic, rather than evidence of remorse for sins, and hence they conclude that absolution would leave these feelings untouched. Others no longer hear people speak about guilt feelings, only about stress, anxiety, and coping—and perhaps about grieving. Have we entered a postguilt era, or are people suppressing guilt feelings as they tune in on current concerns and promises? A few pastors on a regular basis respond to persons' self-exploration and owning of fault with definite words of forgiveness, perhaps in a ritual form, however informal. On the whole, however, this kind of pastoral response is not commonplace, at least among Protestants. Is absolution appropriate only in limited circumstances in the pastoral care of individuals and families? Or is it, rather, a valid aspect of ministry that is neglected and unexamined?

In this chapter I want to show that confession/absolution embodies the evangelical principle of all pastoral care. Yes, baptism and the Eucharist are equally evangelical, but in confession and absolution the focus is more narrowly and exclusively given over to the evangel that removes guilt and so obviates guilt feelings. The ministry of confession/absolution is that part of pastoral ministry that reminds pastors that all of their ministry is at heart evangelical.

In *Pastoral Care in Historical Perspective*, William Clebsch and Charles Jaekle bewail the loss of ritual in pastoral care.[1] William Hulme argues that "to separate the church's means of grace from pastoral counseling would divorce pastoral counseling from its Christian context."[2] Already I have acknowledged my belief that God can give God's grace in any way God desires. Yet I believe that there are designated means of grace that have been effective in the life of God's people. To overlook these means of grace—such as prayer, Scripture, and the sacraments—is not sensible in pastoral care ministry. The ministry of absolution in the context of personal confession of sin is one particular means of grace that has been the center of theological disagreement, but to neglect it debilitates Christian service as a ministry of reconciliation.

Theological Understandings

Confession is not neglected in corporate services of worship, although the response in many liturgies is a general assurance of pardon rather than a definite proclamation of forgiveness in the form of direct address. (There are other problems in this part of corporate worship, which will be discussed later.) The situation is different, however, in pastoral ministry with individuals and families. Rarely does a Protestant minister hear a confession and pronounce absolution. In pastoral ministry with individuals and families the emphasis has been on the personal authenticity and availability of the minister as person to other persons. Certainly this emphasis is sound. But there is a problem. More and more pastors seem to assume that if they can communicate only "I love you," then that will translate clearly into "God loves you." I recall the story of a former professor at Austin Presbyterian Theological Seminary who walked across the campus of the University of Texas one day. A young stranger, possibly a student, accosted him with these words, "Sir, I want you to know that I love you and that God loves you." The professor replied, "Young man, I want you to know that half of what you have told me is good news!"

Yet in the minds of many pastors, use of means of grace such as prayer or a ritual of confession and absolution is associated with being unauthentic, with hiding behind a professional role. I believe that setting the means of grace over against personal authenticity in pastoral care and counseling ministry is a mistake. In fact, when one replaces the pretentious "I love you" with genuine care, human and divine love clearly are brought together.

1. William A. Clebsch and Charles Jaekle, *Pastoral Care in Historical Perspective: An Essay with Exhibits* (Englewood Cliffs, N.J.: Prentice-Hall, 1964).
2. William Hulme, *Counseling and Theology* (Philadelphia: Muhlenberg Press, 1956), 202.

The current tendency of some pastors to distance themselves from religious resources in their pastoral care is based on a popular misunderstanding of insights from psychological disciplines and practice, and unfortunately has become a habit of mind. This is one reason for the neglect of a ministry of absolution in the context of personal confession of sin, reconciliation to God, and reconciliation to one another.

Since the Reformation the ritual of absolution has been a topic of controversy in the Christian churches. Luther himself, while he criticized many aspects of the theology and practice of the church, accepted absolution and "the authority of ministers to absolve from sin."[3] He eliminated any prescription of penance to make satisfaction for sin in favor of a call to live a life of faith. Protestants today differ on whether and how absolution is to be practiced in the church's ministry. Nonetheless, although a host of theological and ministry issues remain unresolved, many churches have made progress in dealing with the controversy. Currently a number of fresh ecumenical developments in theological thought are being put in conversation with contemporary psychological thinking in order to reconstruct and reassess the churches' understanding of confession/absolution as a means of grace.

Psychiatrists and psychologists frequently say that in their conversations with patients they must provide the secular equivalent of confession and absolution or refer patients to clergy who can offer this (in fact they rarely make such referrals). That is, despite our culture's obsession with autonomy, today's secular priests of autonomy are reporting that individual welfare often depends on a human transaction in which one person confesses fault to another, who in turn accepts and provides definite assurance of pardon. Martin Smith puts the matter this way: "The value of disclosing one's innermost and perhaps painful secrets to another person became more intelligible to many after the rise of psychiatry and the counseling movement."[4]

Even though pastors generally realize the importance of listening to persons as they disclose their problems and faultedness, pastors tend to assume that listening is sufficient or that the way to proceed beyond empathy is to guide persons through a problem-solving process. The avoidance of a definite pronouncement of forgiveness to persons may derive from theological questions. It may also relate to uncertainty about the psychological soundness of such a response (for example: Does absolution short-circuit the healing process?). In light of this situation I wish to argue that recent

---

3. Martin L. Smith, *Reconciliation: Preparing for Confession in the Episcopal Church* (Boston: Cowley Publications, 1985), 117.
4. Ibid., 120, 121.

developments in both theological and psychological disciplines call for a reconstruction and reassessment of confession/absolution in pastoral care.

ROMAN CATHOLIC DEVELOPMENTS

Absolution simply is "the pronouncement of remission to the penitent."[5] Since Vatican II there has been a decided shift of emphasis in the categories for interpreting the sacrament of confession and absolution, now called the rite of reconciliation.

To begin, this sacrament is now clearly placed in the context of God's reconciling activity. This means that, while a penitent spirit still is taken seriously, it is not a dominant or exclusive focus of the sacrament. It is God who takes initiative out of a loving desire for reconciliation. Consequently, in the new rite the priest is instructed to "welcome the penitent with fraternal charity, and . . . address him with friendly words." Furthermore, the priest "urges the penitent to have confidence in God."[6] Thus a clear emphasis is placed on the divine desire for reconciliation and power to effect it. The guiding theme of reconciliation also places the rite of absolution in a social context. Because Christians' common life binds them together in a transnatural solidarity, "penance always entails reconciliation with our brothers and sisters who are always harmed by our sins" (*Rites,* p. 344). Because of this social connectedness, the rite of reconciliation is the liturgy whereby "the Church renews itself" (*Rites,* p. 349). To fulfill its purpose in the lives of Christ's faithful people, absolution "must take root in their whole lives and move them to more fervent service of God and neighbor" (*Rites,* p. 347). Although the pronouncement of absolution is a function of the office of the ordained priest, its context is the ministry of the entire church: "The whole Church, as a priestly people, acts in different ways in the work of reconciliation which has been entrusted to it by our Lord" (*Rites,* p. 347).

The structure of this sacrament in the Roman Catholic tradition as now practiced is instructive for ecumenical reflection. Prayer by both penitent and priest is highlighted as essential to preparation and sounds the note of mutuality, which the contemporary church now emphasizes. Then comes the priestly welcome to the person. In contrast to the old style of penance with the priest hidden from view, now priest and penitent face each other in a more social, dialogical style of interaction. Because contrition is vital to transformation of the whole person and because Scripture sheds light on divine mercy and human faultedness, reading the word of God follows

---

5. *Encyclopaedia Britannica, Micropaedia,* 15th ed., s.v. "absolution."
6. *The Rites of the Catholic Church, as Revised by Decree of the Second Vatican Ecumenical Council and Published by Authority of Pope Paul VI* (New York: Pueblo, 1976), 350. (Hereafter in the text this work will be referred to as *Rites.*)

the welcome, or may be suggested as part of preparation for the sacrament. The person confesses sin as completely and openly as possible. In response the priest suggests an act of penance or satisfaction. This is not punishment for sin but honors the principle of justice by prescribing action that corresponds symbolically to the seriousness of the sin. Further, it provides an antidote for human weakness and launches one into new life in Christ. Its social significance is underscored: "This act of penance may suitably take the form of prayer, self-denial, and especially service of one's neighbor and works of mercy. These will underline the fact that sin and its forgiveness have a social aspect" (*Rites*, p. 351). The priest then provides absolution. This is done in these words:

> God, the Father of mercies,
> through the death and resurrection of his Son
> has reconciled the world to himself
> and sent the Holy Spirit among us
> for the forgiveness of sins;
> through the ministry of the Church
> may God give you pardon and peace,
> and I absolve you from your sins
> in the name of the Father, and of the Son,
> and of the Holy Spirit. (*Rites*, pp. 362–63)

Finally, praise is given to God and the person is dismissed.

What is the significance of the structure of this ritual? I suggest that the context of relational reconciliation unifies the whole and gives all the parts an integral relation to one another. Consequently, following Jean Christine Lambert's concept of "action,"[7] I suggest that these elements are not series of actions but essential aspects of a single action. The Roman Catholic rite, then, depicts one interpretation of how Christians are being transformed into the image of Christ, as sons and daughters of God. This means, for example, that a suggested penance is not a work of human merit but is an act symbolizing concretely the way in which God is transforming the person.

Today Roman Catholic theology and practice are in transition—in itself a process of transformation. Protestant stereotypes and fears (for example, that confession of sins reinforces scrupulosity or that penance fosters a "salvation by works" mentality) may be dated. It is time to pitch the sail and test the waters anew for direction in our time.

PROTESTANT DEVELOPMENTS

In general terms, the situation among Protestant churches looks like this: Most provide a corporate assurance of pardon after confession in

---

7. Jean Christine Lambert, *The Human Action of Forgiving* (New York: University Press of America, 1985), 40.

public worship, but have no ritual for personal conferences of the person with a pastor. Those that have a practice of individual absolution see it as a voluntary matter. How do theological tradition and contemporary theological developments shed light on current practice?

Catholic moral theology provides guidance for identifying wrongs to be confessed. The Protestant perspective on human guilt, in contrast, has eschewed attention to specifics in favor of a raised consciousness regarding the pervasive, underlying foundation of human faultedness—and how this sinfulness affects one's relation with God. Profound as the Protestant approach may have been, it has washed ashore on the sands of diffuse, personal conscience. The human condition thus remains detached from particular behaviors and patterns of behaviors that give color and shape to humans' relations with God and neighbor. In fact, to the extent that Protestant pastoral care gives attention to specifics, it has done so by listening to modern psychologies, especially those that emphasize human dynamics and interaction patterns between people. If Protestants are flexible enough to borrow from the psychological disciplines for some concreteness, perhaps they also can learn from their Catholic brothers and sisters.

The concreteness encouraged in confession, however, is not the heart of the matter. On the Catholic side, one finds a process of reenvisioning the meaning of the ritual. On the Protestant side, especially in the liturgical renewal movement, one finds a fresh emphasis on ritual. How can these two be integrated to make a reassessment of absolution possible? Let us begin with a reemphasis on the word, and with a recognition that the ministry of the word is not exclusively preaching or prophecy.

In Scripture the notion of the word has many meanings—from a particular saying of a prophet, to wisdom sayings, to the Word embodied and personified in Jesus Christ. The word, then, is a particular kind of metaphor with many meanings and cannot be contained within a "herald model" of ministry. Accordingly, one can speak of ministry of the word at a *verbal* level, where words of faith are voiced and heard; ministry of the word at a *dynamic* level, where faith is communicated in spirit and in the tone of interpersonal interaction more than in content; and, finally, ministry of the word at a *symbolic* level, where faith is communicated in symbolic acts, formal in the case of ritual and informal as well. Given this understanding, absolution is not an automatic, magical act. For the act to be effective, its meaning must be clear and heard in depth. At the same time, the word is conveyed in sign and act as well as verbally. What is voiced is fully heard when it is embodied.

In the case of confession/absolution, there is an order of worship even for a personal conference. The rite embodies the meaning of the words when, for example, the hand of the priest or minister is outstretched or placed on the person's head. It also works at a verbal level, conveying the content of the gospel addressed to the penitent person. But the person of the minister in relation to the parishioner is not thereby excluded. Not that the priest or minister *as a person* has power to give God to or keep God from anyone; but when personal spirit is congruent with word and act, the word of God is present dynamically. This is why Clinical Pastoral Education and related forms of theological education emphasize the genuine availability of the minister as a person to other persons. The authority of the word spoken is not the authority of a person over another person, but the authority of the truth, the truth of God. The authority of the word dynamically conveyed in interpersonal spirit is the authority of genuineness as God's gift to the minister. The authority of the word embodied in ritual is the authority of a concrete form that evokes and shapes faith. All this can make absolution a powerful communication of the gospel of Jesus Christ, for when the word is fully heard faith is born, and the word creates and gives what it speaks about.

Many Protestants are rediscovering ritual in their corporate worship. This renewal is bound to disclose to them the meaning and power of ritual. Further, this liturgical renewal process is being extended to pastoral care ministry—that is, beyond corporate worship. Modern pastoral care as it emerged in the form of Clinical Pastoral Education was itself a renewal movement in the life of the church. As another such movement, liturgical renewal is beginning to interact with and revitalize pastoral care. It is timely and vital, then, to reconsider the ministry of absolution in the context of personal confession of sin.

Given this broad perspective on absolution in the Protestant movement and Roman Catholic tradition, let us examine briefly several particular traditions: Lutheran, Reformed, Anglican, and Methodist.[8]

Lutheran and Reformed

Lutheran use of absolution in the context of personal confession is so limited that it appears to be a practice reserved for exceptional cases. Lutherans' corporate ritual has two forms, one of which definitely pronounces absolution in contrast to general words of assurance. Luther himself continued to advocate absolution, both corporate and personal. The change he inaugurated with respect to this practice was one of interpretation. Initially Luther viewed confession/absolution as a sacrament; later he grew silent on this question, but he continued to affirm both the priesthood of believers and the church's office of ordained minister as vehicles for such

8. No doubt an examination of Eastern Orthodox thought and practice, which is beyond the scope of this study, would enrich understanding of theological developments.

a means of grace. For Luther, confession was not a matter of trying to recall every sin so that a list would be complete. Instead of a catalog of certain sins, confession was a concrete way of acknowledging that one is a sinner.[9] Thus the Large Catechism says, "When I urge you to go to confession, I am simply urging you to be a Christian."[10] Bonhoeffer believed that the confession of sin to God in the presence of another human being brings about "the public death of the sinner."[11]

Luther had some conviction about the effectiveness of words of absolution. Thus he says:

> If absolution is to be right and effective, it must flow from the command of Christ and must say this: I absolve you and your sins . . . in the name of Christ and by virtue of His command. He has commanded me to tell you that your sins are forgiven. . . . And you are in duty bound to accept this absolution and firmly to believe it not as the word of man but as if you have heard it out of the very mouth of God himself.[12]

Note the kind of dynamic that underlies this proclamation. Whereas many pastors today, if they proclaim any absolution at all, say in essence, "According to your faith your sins are forgiven," Luther proclaims in essence: "This is a personal word for you from God, not from me, so be sure to believe it." The one style of communication makes what is proclaimed depend on one's faith; the other evokes faith on the basis of the truth proclaimed.

Luther set absolution in the context of justification by faith. As Walter Koehler claims, "The practice of individual confession and absolution stands as one of the most clear and concrete pastoral applications of justification by grace." But what has happened? Koehler acknowledges that at the level of practice in Lutheranism today counseling has taken the place of confession, Holy Communion has taken the place of absolution.[13]

How does Calvin contribute to an understanding of the Protestant tradition on the question of absolution? He believed that the Roman Catholic doctrine of penance tortured the conscience, and he eschewed any understanding that repentance is the cause of divine forgiveness. He did, however, enjoin public and private confession of sin before God. He believed that individuals are free to choose their confessor, but he gives the preference

9. Walter J. Koehler, *Counseling and Confession: The Role of Confession and Absolution in Pastoral Counseling* (St. Louis: Concordia, 1982), 48.

10. Cited in ibid., 43.

11. Dietrich Bonhoeffer, *Life Together*, trans. John W. Dobersteing (New York: Harper and Row, 1954), 114.

12. Martin Luther, *What Luther Says: An Anthology*, ed. Ewald M. Plass (St. Louis: Concordia, 1959), 8.

13. Koehler, *Counseling and Confession*, 38, 57.

to pastors, who should be the best qualified. He states: "While the duty of mutual admonition and rebuke is entrusted to all Christians, it is especially enjoined upon ministers." Furthermore, he declares: "It is no common or light solace to have present there the ambassador of Christ, armed with the mandate of reconciliation, by whom [the church] hears proclaimed its absolution." He believed that absolution publicly and privately "sealed" gospel grace in the hearts of believers. Calvin did not believe that a priest forgives sins; rather the confessor "pronounces and declares" them forgiven."[14]

Anglican and Methodist

Anglicans are renewing personal confession. The 1928 *Book of Common Prayer* encouraged personal confession in the rite for visitation with the sick and in one of the exhortations at Holy Communion. The present prayer book contains a separate liturgy for the reconciliation of the penitent. It has two forms. The first follows the 1662 *Book of Common Prayer,* using the words, "I absolve you." The second implores Christ to forgive the penitent through the priest's ministry. In the Anglican tradition this rite is voluntary and encouraged at particular times, namely: (1) during counseling; (2) when persons feel helpless in a cycle of guilt; (3) when persons are returning to church or reaffirming their baptismal vows; and (4) when persons, on their own initiative, desire deeper relationship with Jesus Christ.[15] Its voluntary nature is in keeping with the spirit of Protestantism, which George Bernard Shaw in *St. Joan* defined as "the protests of the individual soul against the interference of the priest between the private man and his God." Clebsch and Jaekle argued that one of the four classic functions of pastoral care—that is, reconciliation—is most open to experimentation and renewed application.[16] This interpretation is supported by both Catholic and Anglican developments.

John Wesley did not write much on the topic of absolution, although he had much to say about means of grace, the witness of the spirit, and the assurance of faith. The reason is simply that Wesley assumed the validity of Anglican practice in his day as reflected in the 1662 *Book of Common Prayer.* His later comments on the priestly office substantiate this. Just as preaching in the Methodist movement was not a substitute for Holy Communion, so for Wesley class meetings did not take the place of personal confession and absolution. Departure from Wesley is not unknown in

14. John Calvin, *Institutes of the Christian Religion* ed. John T. McNeil. (Philadelphia: Westminster, 1960), 3/4:636, 638, 639, 649, 650.
15. Smith, *Reconciliation.* See also Clark Hyde, *To Declare God's Forgiveness: Toward a Pastoral Theology of Reconciliation* (Wilton, Conn.: Morehouse-Barlow, 1984).
16. Cited in Clebsch and Jaekle, *Pastoral Care,* 82.

Methodist history; however, the neglect of confession/absolution among Methodists has no theological basis in the writings or spirit of their founder. In addition to noting a shift in Roman Catholic emphases regarding reconciliation, one must take note of a gap between tradition and practice for many Protestants. In the above survey of selected Protestant groups and of constructive perspectives on an enlarged theology of the word, I have argued that most Protestants can and should reconsider the practice of the ministry of confession/absolution. This does not mean that no serious differences will remain between Roman Catholic and Protestant interpretations. As the context for the practice, nonetheless, reconciliation has emerged as a dominant theme that speaks to Christians in various traditions. Furthermore, the liturgical renewal in Protestantism allows individual confession and absolution to serve as a primary ritual in the cure of souls. But the question then arises: Does pastoral counseling require confession and absolution in ritual form for its completion? To answer this question I want now to put some of these theological reflections in conversation with psychological understanding.

Psychological Analysis

Can the psychological perspective previously introduced help to explain what happens in the ministry of absolution? Can it thus assist us in avoiding a dualism that sets means of grace in pastoral ministry over against personal authenticity? This perspective on psychological functioning provided an account of how symbolic thinking originates in primary interpersonal relationships. The personal images have great power. The early images of self and parent are bigger than life. They are affect-laden. They picture the self's basic ties and integrity and lay the groundwork for all symbolic activity. Cultural symbols gain much of their power because they address these primitive, first images of self and other.

RE-PRESENTING GOD AND COMMUNITY

In a pastoral ministry of the church such as confession and absolution, a human person—a pastor, priest, or other representative—is placed in a symbolic world to re-present God and the community of faith. This world is bigger than life, and on this "stage" is reenacted the divine-human relation. A parentlike figure voices and acts out divine forgiveness by using the words of absolution and the laying on of hands or another gesture. Not just the conscious mind is addressed or affected, but also the underlying world of basic images through which the experience of self and other are known.

What is presented in this rite? Not an understanding of God that is based entirely on infantile images of God, but an understanding of God that reflects divine disclosure in the history of God's people. God remains personal, yet transcends the limits of the particular persons through whom a sense of the personal first emerged into mental functioning. The God presented is not merely the invention of an idiosyncratic, infantile experience. The God of the gospel confronts the whole of one's experience. Consequently, the God present and re-presented in this ministry can correct aspects of one's concept of God, confirm other aspects, and advance understanding of God. Presentation of the God of mercy is essential to the process and cannot be overemphasized. In fact, highlighting God's merciful goodness is the appropriate way to foster genuine penitence and desire for new life.

No reconciliation with God is possible except in Christ, the reconciler (2 Cor. 5:19, 20). In the ministry of reconciliation, pastors or priests can declare absolution because God sees Christ in their stead. It is Christ's own self-offering (sacrifice) that is acceptable. In and through him one's confession as an offering of self becomes acceptable. As Christ is glorified, in him the faithful are glorified and become acceptable. This is the "transfiguration" of the faithful. They receive a new image in God's eye. In Christ, God sees them anew, provoking a new relationship with them. This divine acceptance is a gift that positions the faithful so that they see their own selves anew. Through Christ they are seeing God see them in a new light. This is not narcissism—God is accepting them, not adoring them. This acceptance and reconciliation proclaimed in words and signs of absolution free Christians to adore God.

CHALLENGING THE PERSON'S SELF-IMAGE

The presentation of the forgiving God in this rite challenges the person's self-image. This is why Luther emphasized confession in order to know oneself as a sinner. Unfortunately, some still create a morbid version of this kind of self-image. The possibility proffered in this rite, however, is the discovery of a unique place that is large enough for good and bad self-images, the various selves held together. In daily life one hardly ever perceives a total self, especially because one invests so much energy into a persona. The confession of sin helps to correct this imbalance, diminution, and fragmentation in self-understanding. Through confession, people's sins are, as it were, disarmed, like an enemy. The sins remain in view, but they have lost their hold over those who are forgiven. There is indeed still a split in the spirit and mind—those who are forgiven are radically alienated from that which alienates them from God. But this new split is not like the old, infantile one, where the good and bad images of other and self are cut off from each other. There the feared images, although removed, retain their power via their hiddenness, their secret existence. Here awareness of sin is retained and enlarged while the power of receiving God's love disarms the enemy within. Although in terms of awareness, one's sin is within view, it has no more power to control the one bathed in loving forgiveness than does an enemy who is disarmed. The more one is suffused with this forgiveness, the more one discovers how awareness of sin and disengagement from sin walk hand in hand.

Because of the divine readiness and power to forgive, one need no longer hide the depths of faultedness, of sin and its consequences, from conscious awareness, but can be more self-accepting not only in terms of inner attitude but also in terms of owning faults before others. The confession of sins in the presence of another human being is one step in the direction of being more honest generally with others. The public and private confession of sins fosters the kind of community where people can be freer and more honest with one another and continue to be supported and sustained in the kind of love that the grace of God makes possible.

ADDRESSING NEUROTIC GUILT

What the rite does, then, is to present. It presents an objective reality by projecting it into the transitional space of the sanctuary and soul, where it lures the community and the individual to construct social and subjective freedom on the foundation of the objective freedom provided and proclaimed in the gospel of Jesus Christ.

This analysis calls for a reconsideration of the standard rule that states that the rite of reconciliation is appropriate for dealing with real guilt, but psychotherapy is required for dealing with neurotic guilt feelings. This rule of thumb contains much wisdom, but it oversimplifies the realities of people's lives that are encountered in pastoral ministry. The reason the rule is overly simple is that behavior and guilt feelings flow from basic images and feelings about the self. Among healthy persons the ministry of confession and absolution is not merely to remove the guilt of specific sins in the manner in which one solves a practical problem. The ministry addresses the whole person, the inner self-images. This ministry should certainly help people sustain a healthy self-image, but it should also help to deepen this self-image, opening persons to more profound self-understanding before God. In the case of neurotic guilt, the ministry of confession/ absolution also addresses basic self-understandings. In instances of distorted self-images, this ministry challenges them by presenting the strength and certitude of God's love and mercy. This is one reason why forceful proclamation of absolution generally is more fitting than a bland, overly general assurance of pardon. In neuroses various self-images are maintained in the psyche with a more rigid deliberateness and need than one is likely to realize. Because of this, the ministry of reconciliation needs to be augmented by additional services such as psychotherapy or the healing of memories.

The above psychological account—which explains how a message and an image of God are received at both conscious and unconscious levels of mental functioning—can assist a modern understanding of the theological claim that God forgives sin through the proclamation of the gospel in the power of the Spirit. The ministry of absolution is not a task of rational persuasion, a moment to persuade people against their own resistance to believe God. Although reason and persuasion can aid, they do not heal the breach that one experiences in oneself. According to Calvin: "It is harder for the heart to be furnished with assurance than for the mind to be endowed with thought."[17] Ministries have available to them not only influential words but the power of the Spirit, which communicates not only in words, however important they may be, but also in symbolic acts, in the ritual. The ministry of reconciliation presents the whole act of God's transforming grace to the depth and breadth of the human spirit.

In her analysis of people's representations of God, Ana-Maria Rizzuto claims that transformations in these representations are most likely to occur when people are in crisis or experience other kinds of transitional moments.[18] The typical pastor or chaplain knows well that people, however sophisticated and controlled ordinarily, "regress" in crises with the result that buried guilt feelings rise with great force. At these times old images no longer appear to be adequate, and the struggles of the human spirit open persons to new perceptions and thus to genuine change. An authentic hearing of the good news is possible. Penitence, then, is nothing but the spirit that is no longer holding on to its old ways but has begun to look to God for grace. Although there is a compulsive kind of contrition that glories in itself and has all the marks of a recycled product, there is a vital place for a contrition that helps pave the way to transformation. Accordingly, I suggest that psychological observation supports the theological insight that penitence is a vital dimension of the transformation process.

The main point of this analysis is clear: From a psychological viewpoint the declaration of divine forgiveness in word and symbolic act has enormous power to impart the reality to which it refers.

Implications for Pastoral Care

The first implication of this analysis is that the need for a rite of reconciliation, including a definite absolution, is greater than most pastors and chaplains realize. Far from being peripheral to the thrust of the post-modern world, reconciliation is central. The meaninglessness and nostalgia

17. Calvin, *Institutes*, 3/2:584.
18. Ana-Maria Rizzuto, *The Birth of the Living God: A Psychoanalytic Study* (Chicago: University of Chicago Press, 1979).

common today reflect the kind of alienation that is relational, so the response
to it must lead to reconciliation.

Taking clues from Coleridge and others, Kenneth Burke developed a
dramatistic theory of symbolic action to account for human behavior, a
theory that formulates line-for-line secular equivalents to Christian theology. The two grand movements of human life, in Burke's analysis, have
to do with guilt and redemption, and whatever scheme detracts from this
central matter leads astray.[19]

Although many Protestants have a ritual of confession of sin and absolution or assurance of pardon in their corporate worship, they make no
use of such a ritual in pastoral work with persons. Typically, this means
that private confession of sin and hearing of absolution have no concrete
embodiment in Protestants' personal lives. The complaint that pastors have
no pastors for themselves is heard frequently. One concrete way for ministers to address this problem is to learn to be priests to one another by
using a rite of reconciliation. Without such a practice, ministers rule out
a definite way in which the evangelical heart of their own faith can be
renewed at dynamically critical points in their lives. Ministers who participate in a rite of reconciliation in their own lives have a more nuanced
and clear sense of how to minister to others.

Neglect of this ritual carries a price. To see this one need only examine
what happens without it. In my experience most Protestant ministers are
overly eager to assure people of forgiveness. They jump to assure people
before they have become concrete about the faultedness they want to
confess. It is as though the pastor does not even want to hear a confession.
The ritual of reconciliation precludes such impulsive avoidance and rejec-
tion of people because it establishes the expectation of concrete confession.

Even though a rite of reconciliation evokes concrete confession, there
is a danger that some pastors will use it rather mechanically. There must
be no hurry, for there must be a genuine hearing of one person by another.
When individuals talk to themselves they hardly ever really hear themselves.
Genuine self-listening ordinarily requires another listener. When people
listen to themselves, they typically listen to their fantasies. But when another
person listens intently and is attentive, then individuals truly begin to hear
themselves in what others reflect back to them. The process enables a fresh
experiencing of oneself, one that sometimes occurs when one is caught
off guard. This hearing of oneself through another's hearing is an essential
aspect of the rite of reconciliation.

Can one experience genuine confession of sin without the proclamation
of absolution? The presentation of divine forgiveness in the rite leading

19. Kenneth Burke, *Permanence and Change: An Anatomy of Purpose*, 3d ed. (Berkeley:
University of California Press, 1984).

up to the moment of confession and the expectation of a definite absolution make possible a true sense of penitence and a more complete self-awareness. Although effective pastoral counseling from a dynamic point of view can virtually constitute confession, without a definite ritual that includes absolution, counseling often is little more than catharsis. Hopefully, pastoral care and counseling help persons to distinguish neurotic guilt and habits of mind from genuine sin and appropriate guilt. When this process is more than catharsis—when it entails "discovery," to use John Patton's term[20]—is it not wise to ground and consolidate this discovery in the ritual that enacts the whole process of forgiveness?

The task of integrating the power of the ritual with congruent interpersonal dynamics remains. I say this because I believe that ministry is a matter of verbal, dynamic, and symbolic communication. The relation of all these is of vital importance. God uses the office of ministry as well as the person entrusted with this office in communicating God's grace. Let ministers hope that their interpersonal relations help prepare people for this rite of forgiveness, enliven the process of the rite itself, and sustain the newness of life in Christ given in this rite.

Still, as Daniel Day Williams reminds us, "the healing of the Soul comes from beyond the person and the counselor."[21] This reminder counters two errors. The first I call the deist theory of absolution, the idea that God delegated all forgiveness to priests or ministers and henceforth has nothing to do with it. The second is the claim that persons simply forgive themselves. The ritual opens up the space between self and not-self so that persons begin to realize that forgiveness is not just something that they do to and for their own selves. Without the absolution, they are likely to lose sight of the transcendent dimension in reconciliation.

SYMBOLIC SPACE AND RITUAL DYNAMICS

The above psychological analysis sets forth a clear message for both public and private forms of a ritual of reconciliation. This analysis assumes a distinct kind of symbolic "space" between self and not-self, between inner and outer realities. Ordinarily, ritual opens up and enlarges this space. But just as the rhythmic patterns of interaction between a mother and her infant call for an unhurried and undemanding flow of communication, so effective ritual—ritual that truly enlarges symbolic space—is unhurried. Probably, no church tradition understands this better than the Eastern Orthodox. Ritual always provides a boundary that encloses a symbolic space. The relation of the boundary to the space enclosed must be such that what

---

20. John Patton, *Is Human Forgiveness Possible?* (Nashville: Abingdon, 1985).
21. Daniel Day Williams, *The Spirit and the Forms of Love* (New York: Harper and Row, 1968), 79.

is in the space is held and supported but has freedom of movement. If the boundaries are too rigid or too narrow, they choke and stifle life in the enclosed space. All too often liturgies have become crammed with things to do and no time to be, to exist before God. In many churches the services are dominated by *kronos* in such a way that there is no place for *kairos* to "take place." The brief silences introduced before or following a corporate prayer of confession usually are too short to make a dynamic difference. The liturgy must be slowed down, with more open places of silence where the Spirit of God engages the communal and personal imagination. Silence as part of corporate confession of sin is not simply a matter of personal filling in the blanks so that one's own sins are recited. Rather, the mystery of one's own human fault renders one speechless. This is true as well for the mystery of God's grace, so silence after the absolution provides space to assimilate and sense the wonder of forgiveness.

Likewise, the private rite of reconciliation ought to have time for contemplation and dialogue along with the clearly identified elements of the structure of reconciliation. With time for the more informal dimensions of liturgy, the more formal aspects increase in effectiveness. On first impression, it appears that this observation presents a practical problem, at least for those churches who limited the administration of the rite of reconciliation to the ordained clergy and who have encouraged frequent confessions. But the more effective the interaction in the rite of reconciliation, the less will individuals need to make constant and compulsive use of it.

PENANCE AND CHANGE

Penance in public worship is one clear indicator that worship is set in the midst of life and is to serve life as it glorifies God. In worship the people gather together and one of the things they then do is confess their faulty behavior in daily life as a community and as persons. The forgiveness of sins restores wholesome relation with God, others, and self, and so prepares for mission in the world wherein freedom, justice, and peace are signs of the coming kingdom of God. Yet some persons continue to encounter a gap between forgiveness and transformation in public worship, and forgiveness and transformation in daily life. Can their inherent connection be enhanced in the way the rite of reconciliation is enacted publicly and privately?

I do not expect or advocate that Protestants simply appropriate satisfaction for sins from Roman Catholic practice. For Protestants, human beings cannot satisfy the requirements of divine justice. Nevertheless, Protestants do need to reconsider how the claims of justice are to be honored in confession and absolution. It may well be that in addition to the call for individuals to go and live the Christian life, a dialogue with persons may help them to identify one or more symbolic or reconciling acts that communicate the grateful intent to follow Christ and honor justice on the basis of the mercies granted. One can expect that with genuine penitence and effective proclamation of absolution, persons will discover freedom to forgive others. Thus they can engage in actions with eschatological significance, acts that testify to God's promises. Just as pastoral counseling can help persons clarify what faults need to be confessed, so pastoral guidance can help persons make commitments that reflect the renewed grace in their lives.

From the standpoint of the dynamics of change, it often is better for persons involved to suggest what kinds of changes they would anticipate in light of God's forgiveness in Christ. When pastors and priests take it upon themselves to make suggestions for changes these frequently fail to address specific aspects of a person's life. If, however, persons make their own suggestions, it is easier for them to envision concretely a new self moving in a new direction, one that contradicts specific and obstinate habits of mind and behavior. At least one or two new behaviors—behaviors that represent the mind and action of a new self—can be projected as part of the dialogue that belongs in the rite of reconciliation.

TEACHING OFFICE AND FORGIVENESS

Another task that enriches this ministry is the teaching office. Ministers and priests do well to teach God's mercy, to tutor the imagination so that people have some understanding of what is at stake in such means of grace as the rite of reconciliation. Although this ministry is not primarily a rational process of persuasion, enlightening the mind and setting free the imagination can open the spirits of many to this means of God's grace. It is essential that ministers and priests not substitute rational understanding for ritual reality. To borrow a sentence from a gospel passage, "If your children ask for forgiveness, will you give them an explanation?" Even so, people should be able to envision how the forgiven life bursts out like spring into the creatively ethical life. If persons do not have one individual as both confessor and spiritual guide, then they can seek guidance by participation in a small group or by relating to another person as spiritual guide.

Ministers and priests do the people of God a disservice when they divide the private and the public, the priestly and the prophetic—and when they practice corporate confession and absolution but neglect personal confession and absolution. The motivation for genuine change, the vision for a life that is responsible as well as free and joyful, derives from coming to terms with fault lines that cross both one's personal existence and one's social, political, and cultural coexistence. Christians need corporate and personal confession and absolution.

RECONCILIATION AND PSYCHOTHERAPY

Now, what about the psychological services today that informally seem to resemble elements of the church's ministry? People choose others, whether formally or informally, as their spiritual guides. These relationships often carry with them definite elements of the primary relationships out of which the power of symbolic thought has emerged. In addition to personal choice, our culture provides helping guides, many of them in secular garb. I speak, of course, of psychologists, social workers, psychiatrists, and other counselors. These people have not only professional training, but also a symbolic authority not unlike that of the clergy. This is why they speak of the phenomenon of transference and why their powers often go beyond the powers of rational persuasion. Most concentrate on the psychodynamic dimensions of interpersonal relations, but in that process they discover that basic aspects of self and other can be changed, and that their words have symbolic power far beyond what they may intend. Although they do not officially represent God, they emotionally represent parental figures who have so often formed people's first images of God. I can only suggest that in order to account for such matters they not only resort to systems theory, but also attend to the rite of absolution for a model of what takes place. In any case, both these professionals and the clergy can cooperate with and learn much from each other.

Pastoral care is a ministry of reconciliation. Reconciliation in the context of personal confession of sin and absolution is a vital aspect of this ministry. The ritual dimension of this ministry opens up the interpersonal world for transformation. The definite proclamation of absolution is a powerful dimension of this means of grace, embodies the evangelical spirit of pastoral ministry, opens persons to the full fellowship of God's faithful people, and thus needs to be reclaimed in practice.

CHAPTER 5

Baptism: The Foundation

Many pastors from various churches are expressing new interest in the ministry of baptism. No liturgical alteration has been more radical in the wake of the current liturgical renewal movement than the rites of initiation, including baptism. Not only is this true for the rites of initiation in the Roman Catholic Church, but it is also true for other communions, such as the Presbyterian, which is examining the pastoral significance of new rites of the renewal of baptism.

The new liturgies of baptism claim to be based on a convergence of opinion about the significance of the baptismal practices of the fourth-century church. These practices are held up as the golden age for baptismal and ecumenical understanding. A theological common ground may now be within reach for a mutual recognition of baptism among diverse communions.[1] Yet when the Roman Catholic communion begins suddenly to hold up adult baptism as the norm for an understanding of all baptism, one recognizes both a new appropriation of the tradition and the forceful influence of Christians in the Third World who minister in a "missionary" situation where adult baptism is common.

Indeed, this partnership between fourth-century Christianity and new Third World Christianity appears to be an unlikely one. Can the classical themes, such as burial/resurrection in Christ, speak again in our secular culture? Can they give fresh direction to pastoral ministry? Does this partnership not in fact underscore more boldly the conflict that lurks between theology and pastoral ministry? Is there any precedent in Scripture or early church history for renewal of baptism? And for this book, the

---

1. See *Baptism, Eucharist and Ministry,* Faith and Order Paper no. 111 (Geneva: World Council of Churches, 1982). This work will later be referred to as *BEM.*

perduring question becomes: Is divine grace loosely associated with baptism or is baptism a means of grace? Can one understand baptism as a means of grace without the legalistic framework of some past theology? Previously I have suggested that prayer is the soul of pastoral care and that Scripture heard and received in faith is its substance. This chapter argues that baptism is the foundation or "preface" of pastoral care. This initiation rite re-presents the foundational reality of the Christian faith and life, and consequently it re-presents the basis for pastoral care as an expression of Christian living and service. This foundation is liturgical and sacramental. The nature of this foundation gives enduring strength to pastoral care and sets the limits of its construction. What is the nature of this foundation, and what is the consequent nature and appearance of pastoral care?

In the new baptismal liturgies the human response of faith to the saving grace of Jesus Christ is once again receiving emphasis. In the Baptist tradition, the emphasis still is on the faith of the adult or responsible individual. In those communions that practice infant as well as adult baptism, the faith is as much that of the entire community of faith as it is that of the parents, sponsors, and candidate. Furthermore, for many the rite of baptism does not stand in itself as the rite of initiation but is one of three initiation rites (baptism, chrism or confirmation, and first Eucharist) that help bring faith to fruition. Can we envision a continuity between the infant and the adult such that faith, personal and communal, opens the way for baptism's burial of the old self and resurrection to new life in Christ? Can we discern the way in which adult participation in a renewal ceremony makes baptism a living and transforming memory?

From the vantage point of human experience, the ordinance or sacrament of baptism can be appreciated as an event in "transitional space," that is, as an event that is marked off as different from ordinary events. In this kind of location, as we have seen, poetry, music, story, and the like are born and rehearsed, for consciousness is attuned to unconsciousness. On this stage of the human spirit forgotten associations live again, but may be addressed by different and even new voices. But as a "place" prepared for the soul, baptism is an event that is larger than the literal event. Consequently, it must be understood in terms of what goes before (what is preparatory) and what ensues (follow-up or aftermath) as well as in terms of the dynamics of the event itself. This larger scope is essential for understanding the pastoral dimensions of baptism.

Because the Roman Catholic Church has led the way in liturgical revision of the rites of initiation, its rites of baptism are the primary text for the following analysis and discussion. Although the Orthodox liturgy reflects the pattern of the fourth century, the Orthodox fellowship has neither revised its liturgy nor reexamined its theology in relation to its rites of initiation. For the Roman Catholics there are three rites of initiation: baptism, confirmation, and first Eucharist. For adults and children of catechetical age the three are integrated into one liturgical action. Since Vatican II adult baptism has come to be seen as the norm from which the baptism of infants derives.[2] Accordingly, baptism as part of the rites for the initiation of adults will be examined extensively, and then the implications of the analysis for all baptism in the broader, ecumenical context will be discussed.

Development of Adult Faith

Adult initiation is a process that contains numerous rites and is structured in three major stages inaugurated by rites. The first stage—which is preceded by a period of inquiry in conjunction with the church's evangelization and precatechumenate—begins with the reception of catechumens and encompasses the longest time frame for instruction and maturing of candidates' intention to follow Christ; it may last several years. The second stage is marked by the rite of election, usually on the first Sunday of Lent, when the catechetical preparation is almost complete; this stage constitutes a final season of more complete preparation for the sacraments. The dominant themes for this Lenten stage of preparation are purification and enlightenment. The third stage includes the receiving of the sacraments of initiation and the post-baptismal catechesis or *mystagogia*, which continues throughout Eastertide in order to consolidate the neophytes' faith and assimilate them into the fellowship and mission of the faithful. Although the second and third stages may, when necessary, take place at times other than Lent and Eastertide, they belong to these seasons, and the entire process of preparation has a paschal character.[3]

THE CATECHUMENATE

It is evident that baptism for adults in the Roman Catholic Church is situated in an extensive period of transition and transformation, which involves preparation, participation in sacramental events, and follow-through. As a whole the process has communal, liturgical, pastoral, and personal dimensions.

2. Aidan Kavanagh, "Christian Initiation of Adults" in *Made Not Born: New Perspectives on Christian Initiation and the Catechumenate* (Notre Dame, Ind.: University of Notre Dame Press, 1976), 118.
3. *The Rites of the Catholic Church, as Revised by Decree of the Second Vatican Ecumenical Council and Published by Authority of Pope Paul VI* (New York: Pueblo, 1976), 20–22. Hereafter in the text this work will be referred to as *Rites*. It is assumed that many readers do not have ready access to this book, so the quotations will be extensive.

One advantage of fourth-century Christianity as a model is that in that period preparation for baptism was a rich and complex process in persons' lives. In the newly revised program of the Roman Catholic Church, the essential elements of such preparation are restored. Both catechetical instruction and ritual expression are vital to the dynamics of preparation.

Elements

Acceptance into the catechumenate does not come out of the blue. It is the culmination of a process of inquiry, so that by the time persons enter the catechumenate, they "are required to be grounded in the basic fundamentals of the spiritual life and Christian teaching: the faith first conceived at the time of the precatechumenate; the initial conversion and desire to change one's life and to enter into contact with God in Christ" (*Rites,* p. 24). Personal faith here is envisioned as beginning with a desire and intention that anticipate concrete commitment. The catechumenate process takes this initial disposition and nurtures and strengthens it to the point where personal faith is stable; then baptism can be administered with integrity. The disciplines of the catechumenate make use of four avenues for growth in faith: (1) instruction or formation; (2) the exercise of faith through prayer, seeking Christ in all things, and charity; (3) liturgical rites; and (4) work and service with others in the church's life and witness (*Rites,* pp. 25, 26).

During the catechumenate period, special celebrations of the word of God are held for the catechists' benefit. The goals of these celebrations encompass the same dimensions that are part of the catechumenate as a whole:

a) to implant in their hearts the teachings they are receiving: the unique morality of the New Testament, the forgiving of injuries and insults, the meaning of sin and repentance, the duties Christians have to carry out in the world, and so on;

b) to give them wise teaching on the different aspects and ways of prayer;

c) to explain the signs, actions, and seasons of the liturgy to the catechumens;

d) to lead them gradually into the worship of the whole community. (*Rites,* p. 53)

One can see readily that catechetical preparation has a strong didactic element, which is enriched with spiritual disciplines, including corporate worship and transitional ceremonies, the ethical expression of faith, and cooperative endeavor. The process is designed to engage the whole person. Accordingly, it contains the capacity both to influence behavior and conscious attitudes and to address unconscious elements, including the primary images of one's own self, images of parental and other primary figures, and the way in which one envisions and relates to others. By becoming catechumens, persons identify themselves and are recognized as disciples, as learners intent on discovering, understanding, and following a new way of life:

> During this period, instructions should be given to the catechumens, showing them the whole Catholic teaching. Thus their faith should be enlightened, their hearts should be directed toward God, their participation in the liturgical mystery should be encouraged, their apostolic action should be aroused, and their whole life should be nourished according to the Spirit of Christ. (*Rites*, p. 52)

Inclusion and Integrity

The rite of admittance to the catechumenate is a ritual of welcome and belonging. Catechumens have the right to Christian burial. They "are joined to the Church and are part of the household of Christ" (*Rites*, p. 24). There is a dimension of inclusion even before the catechumenate, for inquirers may be recognized by an informal ceremony of reception (*Rites*, p. 23). This means that from the very beginning of this faith process, a sense of inclusion is clearly and forcefully communicated. As another example, during the catechumenate period, blessings are given. These blessings communicate the love of God and of the church (*Rites*, p. 52). Dynamically, the significance of this phenomenon is that catechumens seek to augment the gift of faith in a supportive context. In fact, personal faith is carried along by the faith community's affirmation of the person. In the context of instruction, prayer, liturgy, inspired acts of love, and common service, such affirmation of the individual promises to have a definite impact on her or his own self-understanding.

The meaning of such welcome and belonging is even more profoundly embodied in the rite of election, usually celebrated on the first Sunday of Lent. At this juncture, catechumens are enrolled among the elect, and are ready for the final period of preparation for the rites of initiation.

This process has much to commend it, but one may ask: Is the whole person always fully engaged in the course of this catechetical preparation, even given the advantage of the dynamics of acceptance and inclusion? If not, then what else should be done? Here the vital significance of integrity surfaces. By integrity I refer to the signs that the individual actually is ready to proceed toward baptism, that the preparatory activities have resulted in some evidence of maturing in faith, and that the person freely desires, chooses, and takes responsibility for the process and its effects. The dynamics of inclusion are balanced by the dynamics of such integrity. Accordingly, "Before the election is celebrated, the candidates are expected to have a conversion of mind and morals, a sufficient knowledge of Christian teaching, and a sense of faith and charity; a consideration of their worthiness is also required. . . . It is thus clear that the election, which enjoys such great solemnity, is the turning point in the whole catechumenate" (*Rites,* p. 27). "Worthiness" or readiness is attested by the priest or catechist, the sponsor, and the peer catechumens. Thus a tension and potential conflict exist between the dynamics of inclusion, which readily acknowledge the person and always anticipate the best, and the dynamics of integrity, which tow the line to concrete evidence of readiness and which must honor the freedom of the individual. Because the process of growth in faith does not always follow a single pattern, some persons take longer than others in their preparation. Implicit in the structure of this process of preparation is the assumption that progress is discussed and assessed periodically so that the integrity of the person and of the church is honored. Consequently, the following structure of the rite of election is like a frozen section of a larger whole, the dynamic process of preparation that has preceded it: "In this rite the Church hears the testimony of the godparents and catechists. After the catechumens reaffirm their intention, then the Church passes judgment on their state of preparation and states whether they may go on to the Easter sacraments" (*Rites,* p. 62).

In light of this process, the significance of extensive instruction and of the special celebrations of the word of God becomes evident. The aim of instruction is to inform the mind. Informed consent is one criterion for freedom of choice, an essential dimension of personal integrity. In the rite of election the integrity of the individual is upheld when the person writes his or her own name into the book of the elect as a free and conscious pledge of fidelity (*Rites,* pp. 26, 27). This aspect of the rite is paradigmatic for all the rites of the adult's preparation for baptism. In each, statements of intent or vows are included, which make personal goals and aspirations overt and public. In terms of integrity, what is crucial at the rite of election is that the person's faith be enlightened or informed and that he or she clearly affirms the deliberate intention to receive the sacraments (*Rites,* p. 62).

Although the structure of the process and of the rites embodies the value of integrity, both personal and corporate, structure as such cannot resolve the inevitable conflicts that arise. Priests, catechists, sponsors, godparents, and others in the church must be committed to encourage questions and free discussion of all issues that arise in the processes of adult inquiry and formation.

PURIFICATION AND ENLIGHTENMENT

The rite of the elect marks the beginning of the period of purification and enlightenment, the final stage of preparation for baptism, confirmation, and Eucharist. This period is less didactic than the catechetical period in the sense that it emphasizes liturgy and spiritual recollection (*Rites*, p. 27). Accordingly, it is directed more toward the transcendent dimension of faith's movement toward the sacraments. The term *election* is used because the church's admission is grounded in God's transcendent election.

The Scrutinies

One can discern a forceful depth dimension in many features of the election and the ensuing period of enlightenment. Take, for example, the simple fact that the candidates now select their own godparents. No longer are these sponsors. Whatever the origin of the term *godparent*, it represents a conflation of "god" and "parent," and calls to mind the reality that children's first image of God is based largely on their mental representations of their parents. But now the candidate is an adult, one who has been inquiring and who has proceeded on a spiritual and moral journey that has arrived at a new place. The individual did not select his or her own parents, but as an adult selects a godparent, who may closely represent a parental image or who may be very different. One's mental image of one's own parents may not be changed in this process, but very possibly it will be repositioned in relation to other mental images, including new ones that are being formed in preparation for baptism. Typically one is not aware of all that is happening internally, but the dynamics of change are no less effective and the symbolic acts such as choosing a godparent no less suggestive, at least to the unconscious.

The depth dimension that is the aim of this phase of the elects' preparation is embodied in the rites of scrutiny (from *scrutari*, to test) and the presentations. Conducted on the third, fourth, and fifth Sundays of Lent, the scrutinies help the elect to examine themselves, increasing awareness of fault and sin, on the one hand, and of strengths and gifts, on the other. The intent is to foster honest and objective self-understanding and discernment, and to arouse in the elect a desire for purification and for Christ's redemption (*Rites*, p. 71). By A.D. 400 there is evidence for three scrutinies. By the sixth century they had increased to seven for symbolic reasons, and this structure endured to the late Middle Ages. The new rites revert to the three scrutinies.

The prayers of exorcism forcefully convey the reality of conflict between good and evil in the person and in the human condition. Evil is understood as a force with a life and intent of its own, in conflict with the powers of light. Indeed, the struggle is far greater than meets the eye of personal consciousness. Too often modern sensibilities resist acknowledging the depths of the experiences of destruction. The vital power of evil calls for a language of images, although the language be unequal to the reality. Thus the satanic image has a profound resonance with the primordial, pervasive, and powerful reality of evil, and it evokes in consciousness these aspects of evil. The dynamics of these rituals work against denial of internal and social conflict, and call persons to acknowledge and address such conflicts. Catechesis and worship that regard exorcism as outmoded may unwittingly contribute to the denial of moral and spiritual conflict at the heart of human existence.

Indeed, the exorcisms of the three scrutinies are not the first exorcisms in the process of preparation. At the rite of the catechumenate, the celebrant breathes toward the face of each candidate and says, "Breathe your Spirit, Lord, and drive out the spirits of evil: command them to depart, for your kingdom is drawing near." Further, the celebrant says to the candidates:

> With the help of God and in response to his call, you have indicated your intention to worship and serve God alone and his Christ.
>
> Now is the appointed time to renounce in public every power apart from God and every form of worship which does not offer him true honor.
>
> Do you reject every power which sets itself up in opposition to God and his Christ? (*Rites,* p. 43)

In addition, minor exorcisms are included as part of the special celebrations of the word of God for the catechumens prior to Lent. So the prayers of exorcism in the rites of scrutiny renew and advance the confrontation with evil in the strength of divine grace. Each scrutiny is centered on a particular gospel story from John: the first on the Samaritan woman, the second on the man born blind, and the third on the rising of Lazarus to life. Thus the prayer of exorcism in the second scrutiny proceeds in this manner. The priest prays:

> Father of mercy,
> you helped the man born blind to believe in your Son and through that faith to reach the light of your Kingdom.
> Free your chosen ones from the falsehoods that surround and blind them.
> Let truth be the foundation of their lives.
> May they live in your light for ever.
> We ask this through Christ our Lord.
> Amen.

The celebrant silently lays his hand on each of the elect and then, extending his hands to encompass all of them, prays:

> Lord Jesus,
> you are the true light that enlightens all men.
> By the Spirit of truth,
> free all who struggle under the yoke of the father of lies.

Arouse the good will of these men (and women) whom you have chosen
for your sacraments.

Grant them to enjoy your light like the man whose sight you once restored,
and inspire them to become fearless witnesses to the faith, for you are lord
for ever and ever.
Amen. (*Rites*, p. 79)

These exorcisms challenge past repression of conflict and ready persons
to engage in the pervasive conflict of good and evil, choosing the good
while acknowledging and taking responsibility for evil. In some individuals
repression is strong and excessive, early conflicts are denied, and the
primitive mental representations of self and primary others are rigid and
relatively fixed. Even though liturgical actions speak in the language of
the unconscious, such rituals are not panaceas for such personal limitations.
Nevertheless, the rituals do challenge; they call on persons to take hold
of faith and to face conflict. Exorcism is liberation in the midst of profound
conflict.

In accepting this challenge some persons seek additional means, such
as psychotherapy, of accepting conflict and modifying self-concept. Indeed,
the only question that might be put to this process is whether the pre-
Lenten catechumenate sufficiently addresses the individual's struggles and
conflict. It is difficult to envision adults making inquiry and submitting to
the disciplines of the catechumenate without their being aware, at some
level, of internal and external conflicts and seeking faith as a way of helping
to resolve those conflicts. What addresses internal and external conflicts
besides the rites? Are the dynamics of conflict embodied in the process of
instruction? Is the encouragement of love and charity toward others balanced
by ways to confront resistance to the good, denial of evil, and temptation?

The Presentations

Two presentations follow the scrutinies. They are the key gifts of the
community of the faithful to the elect: the profession of faith and the Lord's
Prayer, traditionally called the arcana. In these ceremonies, the community
or its representative, the priest, professes faith through the Apostles' Creed
or the Nicene Creed, and prays the Lord's Prayer while the elect listen and
receive. The arcana are handed over (*traducio*) for the elect to learn by
heart and recite (*redditio*) at a later point. This handing down of a tradition
has the dynamic of entrusting new family members with a precious treasure.
Celebrated during the week following the first scrutiny, the presentation
of the profession of faith has the celebrant address the elect in this way:
"My dear friends: Listen carefully to the words of that faith by which you
are to be justified. The words are few but the mysteries they contain are
awe-inspiring. Accept them with a sincere heart and be faithful to them"

(*Rites*, p. 85). The celebrant says the Apostles' Creed alone or with all the faithful; the Nicene Creed also may be used.

The presentation of the profession of faith highlights the role of faith in the elects' reception of the sacraments and in their living of the Christian life. Christianity has long held that the profession of faith has undisclosed power, and one purpose of catechismal preparation is to help candidates for baptism to catch the sense and meaning of this new reality in their lives. In his catechism at Jerusalem, for example, St. Cyril taught, "Make clean your vessel that you may receive more grace. For though the remission of sins is granted to all alike, the communication of the Holy Spirit is granted in proportion to the faith of each." Or again, "If you pretend, men will indeed baptize you, but the Spirit will not baptize you, but if you approach with faith, men will minister to you visibly, but the Holy Spirit will bestow upon you what is not visible."[4]

As a concrete act of presenting the faith to the elect, the community's profession of faith hands on a long-standing and living tradition, a tradition and living truth that enlighten the elect. Such illumination is an essential resource in the war of good and evil, and opens the way for the moment when the elect profess their own faith publicly, thus declaring on whose side they choose to stand in life's spiritual and moral conflict. The presentation of the creed signals a preparedness to receive. Later, on Holy Saturday, the elect make their own profession of faith, reciting one or both creeds.

During the week following the third scrutiny the believing community also presents the Lord's Prayer, and so testifies to the place of prayer in the Christian life. This presentation invites the elect to internalize the prayer and to pray it until their very lives embody and express this prayer. The deacon invites the elect forward, and the celebrant introduces and prays the Lord's Prayer, and then explains its meaning and significance in a homily (*Rites*, p. 88).

These special gifts are the best that the community has to offer in expression of its love, acceptance, and hope. These nonmaterial gifts can be given only in events and only through the material body as the faithful raise their voices to express the energy and meaning of the spirit. Because of this I believe that it is preferable to have the entire congregation voice the creed and the Lord's Prayer.

At the end of the period of purification and enlightenment, on Holy Saturday, the elect are asked to refrain from unnecessary work, to pray, and to fast. This is a moment for intensifying all that has gone on before

4. Quoted in R. Burnish, *The Meaning of Baptism: A Comparison of the Teaching and Practice of the Fourth Century with the Present Day* (London: SPCK, 1985), 8.

and for strengthening and readying personal faith for baptism. Select rites may be celebrated before the Easter Vigil (*Rites,* p. 28).

The Faith Community's Preparation

The participation of the community in the preparation of adult faith indicates that the latter does not stand alone. The process involves joining the faith of the community with the faith of the individual: "The initiation of catechumens takes place step by step in the midst of the community of the faithful. Together with the catechumens, the faithful reflect upon the value of the paschal mystery, renew their own conversion, and by their example lead the catechumens to obey the Holy Spirit more generously" (*Rites,* pp. 20, 21). Thus the interpretative framework envisions Lent as a double preparation: It prepares the candidates and it prepares the community of the faithful for participation in the life of the risen Lord Jesus Christ.

The community's welcome, inclusion, affirmation, and support are an exercise of the community's faith. As preparing individuals participate more and more in the worship, life, service, and witness of the church, the mutuality of their faith interacting with that of the faithful manifests itself. The newly budding faith of the catechumens stimulates the faith of Christians already initiated into the life and ministry of the church, just as the faith of Christians encourages and promotes the catechumens in their new faith and first love.

This mutuality and congruence of faith are especially evident in Lent, for then the community of faith both guides the elect and prepares its own faith for renewed participation in the wonder of the gospel of Christ: "Both in its liturgy and in its liturgical catechesis, Lent is a memorial or a preparation for baptism and a time of penance. It renews the community of the faithful together with the catechumens and makes them ready to celebrate the paschal mystery which the sacraments of initiation apply to each individual" (*Rites,* p. 26). During Lent the faithful are to renew their own lives with penance, faith, and charity in an exemplary way (*Rites,* p. 32). In the presentations the community offers its faith to the elect and shares it with them, entrusting, passing it on, and in effect conjoining the faith of the community with that of its new members. The presentations of the creed and the Lord's Prayer are communal acts—acts made in unison by a gathered community. Here the community acts as a body, is one. Such acts approximate the notion of a "group mind," if you will. A gathered community acting and thinking together is aware subliminally of the world-wide unity of many communities in diverse times and places. The gathered community is in touch with this organic unity and in touch with the transcendent unity of the communion of saints. Corporate acts such as the presentations convey directly to the unconscious mind of new members the rich reality of communal faith, and witness to the profound mysteries treasured in this faith.

Even if there are no candidates for baptism at Easter, the community renews its own faith by recalling baptism in the Easter Vigil.

The faith of the community is also embodied in its representatives: the bishop, the priest, the catechist (if different from the priest), the sponsor, and the godparent. The bishop oversees the entire process of preparation and initiation. Hopefully, he himself celebrates the rite of election and the sacraments of initiation at the Easter Vigil. Priests attend to the pastoral care of catechumens and provide instruction with the help of deacons and catechists (*Rites*, p. 33). A sponsor accompanies the candidate who requests admission as a catechumen. This person or another "delegated by the local Christian community and approved by the priest" serves as godparent during the period of purification and enlightenment. Such a person is to be close to the candidate and set an example of faith:

> It is his responsibility to show the catechumen in a friendly way the place of the Gospel in his own life and in society, to help him in doubts and anxieties, to give public testimony for him, and to watch over the progress of his baptismal life. Already a friend before the election, this person exercises his office publicly from the day of election when he gives his testimony about the catechumen before the community. His responsibility remains important when the neophyte has received the sacraments and needs to be helped to remain faithful to his baptismal promises. (*Rites*, p. 33)

In these ways the faith of the community is conjoined with the faith of the adult candidates who are preparing for baptism. The value of the individual person, the indispensable role of the church, and the essential importance of faith are taken seriously and vigorously upheld. The various dimensions—pastoral, liturgical, social, ethical, cognitive and affective— convey that this preparation is a ministry intended to claim the whole person and community for Christ. The word of God embodied in Scripture and in liturgy is vigorously attended to, and the call to follow Christ in daily life is not neglected. Consequently, when the candidates are brought to baptism, all baptized persons are called to remember and celebrate their own baptism as well as welcome the candidates into the sacramental life of the church.

At the level of social and liturgical interaction, the community's faith is clearly a gift to the individual and the individual's faith is a gift and blessing to the community. But is the full reality of faith as the transcendent gift of God sufficiently articulated in the structure of this process of preparation and its rituals? There is no suggestion that individuals create their own faith out of nothing or that they produce their faith solely by their own determination, effort, and will power. For example, in the rite of the catechumenate the priest says to the candidates:

> God enlightens every man who comes into the world. . . . You have followed his light. . . . You are called to walk by the light of Christ and to trust in his wisdom. He asks you to submit yourself to him more and more and to believe in him with all your heart. This is the way of faith on which Christ will lovingly guide you to eternal life. Are you ready to enter on this path today under the leadership of Christ? (*Rites,* p. 42)

Clearly, personal faith is vital to receiving salvation as God's gift, and one is called to look to Christ. Yet the dynamic of looking to God for faith itself as God's gift is not set forth. So the mysterious action of God, offering and instilling faith, is not emphasized as strongly as I think it could be. Somehow faith is in the hands of the church and the individuals who seek its fellowship; with this faith persons look to Christ and then the mysterious grace of God is imparted sacramentally. It may be assumed that divine grace is preveniently given and that faith is a gift from God that—although received through this and similar processes—is not fully regulated or apprehended through the system; but the gracious action of God as such prior to the mystery of grace in the sacraments is not emphasized. Consequently, the preparation as a process of assimilation is more evident than is preparation as a process of radical discovery.

The Rites of Initiation

The stages of preparation culminate in the rites of initiation—rites of transition from an old understanding of God and self to a new understanding. It remains now to examine and analyze the images in the rite of baptism and the other rites of initiation as the core of this transitional period and its transformations. Baptism is a *pascha,* a passage, from one world to another, from the kingdoms of this world to the kingdom of God, from the monologue of self-salvation to the music of a new song. As Alexander Schmemann, a member of the Eastern Orthodox church, notes, "Baptism is not a magical act adding some supernatural powers to our natural faculties. It is the beginning of life eternal itself, which unites us here in 'this world' with the 'world to come,' makes us even now in this life partakers of God's Kingdom."[5]

BAPTISM

The rite of baptism commences with the completion of a time of preparation. The celebrant calls the candidates and godparents to the font

5. Alexander Schmemann, *Of Water and the Spirit: A Liturgical Study of Baptism* (London: SPCK, 1976), 42.

and addresses the congregation, soliciting their prayer for the candidates participating in this sacrament. Then follows a litany, the blessing of the water, the renunciation of Satan, anointing with the oil of catechumens, and the profession of faith. Finally comes the baptism itself by infusion or pouring in the name of the Trinity. Before confirmation there are additional rites: anointing after baptism in the event that confirmation does not proceed immediately after baptism, clothing with the white garment, and the presentation of the lighted candle. In confirmation the celebrant addresses the neophytes, prays, and then after a moment of silence lays hands on all to be confirmed and prays over them. Then, while each godparent places a hand on a neophyte's shoulder, the celebrant addresses each candidate by name and anoints the forehead with chrism. Finally, the neophytes participate in their first Eucharist.

Let us examine the celebration of baptism in more detail. The litany begins:

> Lord, have mercy.   Lord, have mercy.
> Christ, have mercy.   Christ have mercy.
> Lord, have mercy.   Lord, have mercy.

The litany continues with petitions for Holy Mary, Mother of God, and a host of saints to pray on behalf of all gathered in worship. Remarkably, this is the first time that any prayer, beginning with the inquiry and admission into the catechumenate, has called on this sacred panoply, which includes "all holy men and women." The litany continues with prayers for mercy; for deliverance from evil, sin, and death; and for salvation by the coming, death, and rising of Christ, and by the gift of the Holy Spirit. In this litany the people pray, "Give new life to these chosen ones by the grace of baptism." It should be noted here that baptism itself is deemed a "grace." The litany introduces the salient themes: forgiveness; deliverance; and new life through the incarnation, death, and resurrection of Christ, and the power of the Holy Spirit.

The blessing of the water is a prayer addressed to God the Father. It begins, "Father, you give us grace through sacramental signs which tell us the wonders of your unseen power." Here the water is not grace as such but a visible sign of God's unseen power. The prayer recalls the significance of water in the drama of creation and redemption. Then the prayer continues, "Father, look now with love upon your Church and unseal for it the fountain of baptism." What is meant by this image that the water is sealed and by appeal to a divine action that unseals the water? Is it not significant that such language follows the act of recollecting or remembering God's presence and deeds with respect to water? The prayer asks God to give to the water the grace of Christ and to cleanse humanity. After the celebrant touches the water with his right hand, he asks the Father with the Son to send the Holy Spirit upon the water. The climax of the prayer is this petition: "May all who are buried with Christ in the death of baptism rise also with him to newness of life (*Rites,* pp. 95–98).

The blessing of the water is a kind of reappropriation of water as gift. It already is one of God's gifts in creation. Now this gift is reappropriated and assigned an added significance. This heightened significance is constructed by the anamnesis—a review of events made meaningful by the mystery of water and a reinterpretation of them as part of the redemption enacted in baptism. Thus the blessing of the water sets forth a panoply of signification. The meaning of particular events is reconceived. For example, the Exodus is transvalued so that now it is an image of the freedom from sin wrought in baptism.

The blessing of the water establishes a new relationship between the water and the people of God. Clearly now the water is blessed with the presence and power of the Spirit. Perhaps its "unsealing" is an action whereby the Spirit discloses the fullness of meaning and force present in this water. Remembrance drives the human spirit to this destiny: an unsealing, an epiphany, the creation of a new context or framework in which to see and relate to this water as the vehicle for communion with God.

In this way worshipers are induced to be attentive to the water, which no longer is "mere water," an external substance, but now is conveying the love of God, the grace of Christ, and the power of the Holy Spirit.

Once the water is blessed and its reality made manifest through divine action responding to the prayerful word, the rite proceeds with the renunciation. Several variations can be used, but the simplest is the following:

CELEBRANT: Do you reject Satan and all his works and all his empty promises?
ELECT: I do. (*Rites,* p. 98)

In the fourth century the elect faced west—the direction of sunset and ensuing darkness—during this renunciation. They confronted the enemy of God, the forces of evil, consciously and intentionally, and rejected them.

This action is a reaffirmation and an intensification of a previous intention and growing conviction. The image of dying with Christ, introduced in the opening litany, is now filled out with the context of a spiritual and moral warfare or conflict. The elect abandon and eschew one loyalty and servitude in order to avow a new allegiance and service.

The anointing with the oil of catechumens precedes the profession of faith as a moment when the elect receive added strength to take this next step (*Rites,* pp. 95, 99). The symbolism is that of oil as a medicine to augment health and strength. The catechetical and enlightenment experiences have been more than instruction—they have been therapy. The elect are anointed on the breast or on both hands.

The celebrant addresses each candidate by name, asking if he or she believes in God the Father, in Jesus Christ, and in the Holy Spirit, using the Apostles' Creed and dividing it into three parts. To each of the three questions, the candidate affirms, "I do." At this moment, finally, the candidates own and profess the church's faith as their own. The creed summarizes the substance of the Christian faith, which the candidates affirm and appropriate. The allegiance is public, conscious, and intentional, and it is made after a time of significant involvement in learning, praying, and living in light of the faith.

After the profession of faith the candidate or candidates are baptized by immersion or infusion, the water poured over each candidate three times, once for each member of the Holy Trinity. In the fourth and fifth centuries, the formula was passive, "You are baptized . . . ," and so it remains today in the Orthodox tradition. By the eighth century, the Western formula was in the active voice. Also, before the eighth century the threefold baptism took place as three immersions, one after each "I believe" was given in response to each section of the creed. Later, the threefold interrogation and profession of the creed was placed before the act of baptism itself. In this act the person is washed in the purifying and life-giving water as it conveys the reality of God's total and complete mercy. Traditionally, the Roman Catholic Church has affirmed that "original sin, personal sin and the punishment for sin are expiated in baptism, provided the recipient presents no obstacle to this operation of grace by the disposition of his will."[6] The new adult rite, as we have seen, places more emphasis on active faith. In this baptism the person is conformed to the death and resurrection of Christ (Rom. 6). He or she is born anew of water and the Spirit. Submersion in the water removes one from the old life and inducts one into the new life that flows from the grace of God and allegiance to God. For many of the church fathers, baptism was both tomb and womb. According to John Chrysostom,

> After this anointing the priest makes you go down into the sacred waters, burying the old man and at the same time raising up the new, who is renewed in the image of his Creator. It is at this moment that, through the words and the hand of the priest, the Holy Spirit descends upon you. Instead of the man who descended into the water, a different man comes forth, one who has wiped away all the filth of his sins, who has put off the old garment of sin and has put on the royal robe.[7]

6. *New Dictionary of the Liturgy* (London: Geoffrey Chapman, 1967), s.v. "baptism."
7. John Chrysostom, *Baptismal Instructions*, ed. and trans. Paul W. Harkins Ancient Christian Writers 31 (Westminster, Md.: Newman Press, 1963), 52.

After baptism the celebrant addresses the neophytes:

N. and N., you have become a new creation
and have clothed yourselves in Christ.
Take this white garment
and bring it unstained to the judgment seat of our Lord Jesus Christ
so that you may have everlasting life. (*Rites*, p. 102)

When the celebrant says "Take this white garment . . . ," the godparents place the garments on the neophytes. In their new garments the neophytes affirm what they have heard, saying "Amen." Then the godparents light candles from the Easter candle and hand them to the neophytes. The celebrant says:

You have been enlightened by Christ.
Walk always as children of the light
and keep the flame of faith alive in your hearts.
When the Lord comes, may you go out to meet him
with all the saints in the heavenly kingdom.

The newly baptized respond, "Amen."

Situated as an integral aspect of conversion, baptism celebrates the rebirth of the individual and of the community. As an ordinance or sacrament of the church, it cleanses and renews personal and corporate existence before God. The feast of dedication—of the cleansing of the Temple—is an appropriate image (John 10:22), especially since the Koine term derives from *kainos* (new, fresh in quality, unused, unworn). The individual is baptized; the community celebrates; members of the community remember their baptism; and the community thereby is renewed, re-membered, and reconstituted—born again. Accordingly, A. Kavanaugh can write, "Less do these same norms present the sacraments as discrete events geared to phases in an individual's life than as stages in the process of ecclesial living together under the aegis of Jesus Christ dying and rising continually among his faithful ones."[8]

CONFIRMATION

The confirmation follows. As at the oil of catechumens, the emphasis is on God's gift of strength: "The promised strength of the Holy Spirit, which you are to receive, will make you more like Christ, and help you to be witnesses to his suffering, death, and resurrection. It will strengthen you to be active members of the Church and to build up the Body of Christ in faith and love." The celebrant lays hands on the candidates and prays:

8. Aidan Kavanagh, "Christian Initiation of Adults," 119.

All-powerful God, Father of our Lord Jesus Christ,
by water and the Holy Spirit
you freed your sons (and daughters) from sin
and gave them new life.
Send your Holy Spirit upon them
to be their Helper and Guide.
Give them the spirit of wisdom and understanding,
the spirit of knowledge and reverence.
Fill them with the spirit of wonder and awe in your presence.
We ask this through Christ our Lord. (*Rites,* pp. 103, 104)

Note that the expectation and prayers for strength now culminate in this prayer to an all-powerful God to give the Holy Spirit. This is understood as a lasting gift, one that strengthens and guides for the lifelong struggle between God and the forces of evil within and without.

As the godparent places the right hand on the candidate's shoulder, the celebrant makes the sign of the cross with chrism on the forehead and says, "N., be sealed with the Gift of Holy Spirit." After the neophyte's "Amen," the celebrant adds, "Peace be with you," and the neophyte says, "And also with you."

This is the first priestly act of the neophyte. He or she now is one who is confirmed as a member of Christ's body, and so participates in the priesthood of believers. This is a clue to the nature of baptism and confirmation: They are a distillation of the conversion process, an intensification of its essence via symbolization. Baptism and confirmation distill in events what has been occurring already as a process. In relation to priesthood, this means that the neophyte already has been learning to minister and has ministered so that with baptism the reality of this new ministry is fully recognized and displayed in the sign of peace.

On what basis is such a ministry and mutuality founded? When Jesus came up from the waters of baptism, the Spirit in the form of a dove descended on him, strengthening him for his temptation and ministry. Likewise, the anointing with oil symbolizes the gift of the Holy Spirit, sealing the baptized as Christ's own and strengthening them for their ministry. This sealing with oil represents the unchangeable effect of baptism (*Rites,* pp. 4, 5).

FIRST EUCHARIST

Accordingly, during the general intercession that follows as part of the Eucharist, the neophytes take part in the ritual for the first time. Some of them bring the gifts to the altar. The neophytes and the godparents are mentioned in the eucharistic prayer. The neophytes together with godparents, parents, spouses, and catechists receive Communion under both species (*Rites,* pp. 102–5). Thus they participate in what is sometimes referred to as *the* sacrament, the thanksgiving that embodies Christians' destiny in Christ.

In summary, consider the vision of John Chrysostom:

> As soon as they come forth from those sacred waters, all who are present embrace them, greet them, kiss them, rejoice with them, and congratulate them, because those who were heretofore slaves and captives have suddenly become free men and sons and have been invited to the royal table. For straightaway after they come up from the waters, they are led to the awesome table heavy laden with countless flavors where they taste of the Master's body and blood, and become a dwelling place for the Holy Spirit. Since they have put on Christ himself, wherever they go they are like angels on earth, rivalling the brilliance of the rays of the sun.[9]

The transformation that is the result of the conversion process culminating in the celebration of baptism and the other rites of initiation is an internal change precisely because it is a relational change: a change in relation to God and in relation to the community of faith, and consequently in relation to one's own self. On the relationship to the community, Reginald Fuller writes, "The resurrection appearances created the community. After hearing of the kerygma and faith, baptism is the means by which God inserts new members into the already existing community."[10] To think of this productively, one should envision God as the one who acts and the church as the community that celebrates and receives the new members. A new self rises in baptism, a new person with a fresh image of God and of self, a new vision of others, and a new status. The dying of an old self-concept and the emergence of a new self-understanding must be deeper than a conscious self-image. This death and rebirth reverberate to the unconscious; they even affect one's image of one's own body and bodily existence as part of self-understanding. In some cultural situations, this rebirth process involves taking a new name as a concrete representation of a new identity. All this is upheld and will be nurtured in the new context of membership in the community of faith, effected through baptism.

The liturgical power of baptism in the context of initiation rites is rooted in the existential and communal realities of the conversion process. The conversion process is energized and guided by anticipation of its concrete culmination in baptism, membership in the church, and new life before God through participation in the church's worship, fellowship, and mission in the world. One may speak legitimately, then, of baptism as a means of grace in that baptism is a dynamic lure for the conversion process, effects

9. Chrysostom, *Baptismal Instructions*, 53.
10. Reginald Fuller, "Christian Initiation in the New Testament," in Kavanagh, *Made, Not Born*, 13.

entrance into the life of the church, and is itself a dramatic vehicle for the rebirth of individual and community.

POSTBAPTISMAL CATECHESIS

In the main, this is the period from the paschal feast and the rites of initiation to Pentecost. The neophytes are to be integrated into the life of the community of faith. At Sunday masses throughout Eastertide, they have a special place in the worshiping congregation, and continue to be mentioned in the homily and general intercessions. At the end of this period, a celebration in accordance with local custom is held. Finally, on the anniversary of their baptism the neophytes are encouraged to gather together again to celebrate and to gain strength from one another. During this period godparents continue to support neophytes in their Christian growth after the rites of initiation (*Rites,* p. 6). In this fashion a follow-up period consolidates the entrance into the new life in Christ and calls for a regular celebration of this unique event and process. The *mystagogia,* "postbaptismal catechesis," then, is a miniperiod that embodies the fact that all of the Christian life follows from this conversion and new birth. The new life in Christ reframes one's self-understanding and understanding of God. Centered in baptism, the rites of initiation form a foundation for the living of the Christian way that flows from this new comprehension of the relation of God, self, and others. It is little wonder that Raymond Burnish sees the new rite for adults as "new wine" in the Roman Catholic Church.[11]

After the elaborate catechetical process culminates in the rites of initiation, any follow-up stage is anticlimactic. Yet the question to consider is whether the proposed *mystagogia* is an adequate closure to all that has gone before it and a sufficient opening to all that is to come in Christian faith, fellowship, and service. It is not a question resolved by extending the time for the *mystagogia*. The *mystagogia* is a time of consolidation by way of reflection on the rites of initiation and their meaning, a time of full integration into the community of faith. The reflection during Lent, the time of enlightenment, had the character of anticipation. Now the neophytes are in a position to reflect back on the fullness of the sacramental experience. Such reflection—a reflection on conversion—in principle has potential for a depth not achieved in anticipatory reflection. As Kavanagh remarks, "At this point sight returns; new things are said that were before unspeakable, new things are seen that were always there."[12] The full exercise of such reflection calls for more than attending mass as a recognized group. It calls

11. Burnish, *Meaning of Baptism,* 143.
12. Kavanagh, "Christian Initiation: Tactics and Strategy," in Kavanagh, *Made, Not Born,* 3.

for the mutual dialogue possible in small group discussions and for personal meditation. Such forms of reflection should make up part of the normative expectations for the mystagogia along with continued participation in the Eucharist.

In the past a ceremony of milk and honey has been a part of initiation rites from time to time. Perhaps such a celebration could be revived and transferred back into the *mystagogia,* where the symbolism is that of new babes in Christ being nurtured by the word of God. In any case, given the radical revisions in the preparation for the rites of initiation of adults and in the rites themselves, the mystagogia could be developed more creatively beyond the suggestions in *The Rites of the Catholic Church.*

Psychological Reflection on Baptismal Images

The conversion process culminating in the rites of initiation trumpets and harbors many images. Together they form a richly textured background and context for the central symbol: the waters of baptism. Sacraments, we must remember, present an outward sign of an inward grace. The outward sign brings the grace to consciousness and also anchors the grace in the unconscious mind. The material of the sign, in this case running water, receives a new significance. It is not "merely" water, but is blessed, consecrated, reflected on, and re-visioned with the eyes of faith. From a human point of view this is an act of the imagination. To cite Immanuel Kant, for example:

> The imagination (as productive faculty of cognition) is very powerful in creating another nature, as it were, out of the material that actual nature gives it. We entertain ourselves with it when experience becomes too commonplace, and by it we remold experience, always indeed in accordance with analogical laws, but yet also in accordance with principles which occupy a higher place in reason. . . . Thus we feel our freedom from the law of association (which attaches to the empirical employment of imagination), so that the material supplied to us by nature in accordance with this law can be worked up into something different which surpasses nature.[13]

Two features of the meaning of the sacramental in Christian faith are vital: (1) that this faith avoids the extremes of materialism and Gnosticism; and (2) that this faith balances personal appropriation and communal presentation. The means of grace and pastoral care as the mutual participation in these means eschew the lackluster materialism and positivism of modern secularity and at the same time define an alternative to every gnostic way

13. Immanuel Kant, *Critique of Judgment,* trans. James Haden (New York: Hafner, 1968), sec. 49.

of salvation, every pure interiority, every idolization of fantasy or special knowledge. In fact, in sacraments the material becomes the means of the spiritual grace. The means of grace call for a corporate and personal positioning in but not of the senses. Personal participation in the community's transitional or liturgical reality strengthens the person's capacity to celebrate, to play, to be at home in this transitional space, and to maintain a flexible balance of internal renewal and external behavior. Personal identity, formation, and ethical praxis require the celebration, organization, and service of the community as the context in which they are constituted and nourished. Communal faith permeates and quickens individual faith. In this light one can see that a critical limitation of Kant's philosophical analysis above is its treatment of imagination as if it were a function of the individual mind or of some abstract group mind.

Also with respect to personal appropriation of communal presentation, the concreteness of the symbolic acts in the rites is vital. Recent psychological research suggests that the memories of normal subjects are more concrete than those of depressed persons. The latter tend to remember events in relatively general terms, while the former remember a greater number of specific features of particular events.[14] Ritual that is replete with concrete symbols enriches the human spirit, and may be needed especially by persons whose memories could benefit from great stimulation. When Martin Luther was depressed, we might recall, he resorted to the memory of his baptism. One function of the brain's limbic system is the integration of the novel with what is already known: "Metaphorical and imagistic language open multiple dimensions of meaning. They set off trains of association. . . . Imagistic words move directly into the limbic process of incorporating new experience with ongoing meaning."[15]

Just as art, music, and other cultural phenomena are transitional, so one can posit that liturgical reality is a form or manifestation of transitional phenomena. This reality is neither material in such a manner that it excludes the nonmaterial nor nonmaterial in such a way as to exclude the material. Rather it represents a mode of understanding reality as a dynamic crossing over of one into the other. This transitioning is the salient characteristic of reality such that the question of internal or external loci is decentered. The centrality of liturgical reality is plain in those theological understandings that declare that the promise and transformation of the gospel are reenacted and actually occur in the liturgical event. But any such theological claim, while it can be praised for its appreciation of corporate worship,

14. See J. Mark G. Williams, *The Psychological Treatment of Depression: A Guide to the Theory and Practice of Cognitive Behaviour Therapy* (London: Croom Helm, 1984).
15. James B. Ashbrook, "The Complex Clarity of Pastoral Therapy: The Perspective of a Pioneer," *Journal of Pastoral Care* 43, no. 4 (Winter 1989): 368.

needs to portray the dynamic relationship between liturgical reality and everyday reality, including ethical transformation in the world beyond worship—for God is not confined to humanly designated sacred spaces.

Liturgical reality intensifies ordinary experiences by compressing the whole into a condensed representation. Thus baptism represents the transformation discovered in Christian living. Baptism inducts one into the life of transforming faith and enacts a paradigmatic portrayal of the entire drama of God's salvation. Although there is one paradigmatic action—the application of water in the name of the Father, the Son, and the Holy Spirit—several images are required to elaborate its meaning. Ecumenical dialogue has highlighted the following images: participation in Christ's death and resurrection (Rom. 6:3-5; Col. 2:12); washing away of sin (1 Cor. 6:11); new birth (John 3:5); enlightenment by Christ (Eph. 5:14); reclothing in Christ (Gal. 3:27); renewal by the Spirit (Titus 3:5); salvation from the flood (1 Pet. 3:20, 21); exodus from bondage (1 Cor. 10:1, 2), and liberation into a family without unjust divisions.[16] Images such as cleansing from sin and dying and rebirth are essential as partial but penetrating perspectives on the significance of baptism and of human transformation. No one image suffices, so it is not prudent to hail one and marginalize another, as some commentators now are prone to do. The various images keep alive the one action and all it represents, prevent it from being reified and imprisoned within one concept. They enable the sacramental act to keep on speaking.

Implications for Pastoral Care

When built on the foundation of baptism, pastoral care is dynamic. It ritually and interpersonally addresses the dynamics of human conflict.

Standing on the foundation of baptism as initiation into the transformed and transforming life, pastoral care must give attention to the ways in which God is represented, not merely in conscious beliefs but also in the dynamics of emotional depths. Ana-Maria Rizzuto believes that "God as a transitional representation needs to be recreated in a developmental crisis if it is to be found relevant for lasting belief."[17] I already have taken a position that celebrations such as baptism should not be interpreted primarily in relation to stages of individual development. Even so, the transformation process enacted in baptism and demonstrated in particular in the normative structure of the rites of initiation for adults provides a model for the way

16. *BEM*, 2.
17. Ana-Maria Rizzuto, *The Birth of the Living God: A Psychoanalytic Study* (Chicago: University of Chicago Press, 1979), 208.

in which human representations of God are re-created in such transitional times. In times of stability, ritual tends to help confirm and consolidate one's inner view of God. In times of crisis or transition, the same ritual tends to help one to rework or remold one's inner vision of God. At these times, one sees and hears new elements or a new gestalt in the ritual experience.

Ritual reality does not eliminate conflict, emotional or otherwise, but it often channels energies in a new direction. The renunciation of evil and profession of faith in baptism are not unlike rational-emotive techniques as a way of escaping the dominance of a distorted self-image (or, in terms of cognitive therapies, the dominance of irrational ideas) and accepting a new basis for self-understanding (the humanistic perspectives that usually undergird rational-emotive therapy define this new basis as rational views of self and one's situation). The baptismal ritual has the advantage of being set in a group context and process, and is structured so that the transformation process has a clear beginning, middle, and end. As designed, this process combines cognitive work with emotional force, a significant feature of rational-emotive therapy and related cognitive approaches to psychotherapy. Still, in the baptismal liturgy, human transformation is made to coincide with entrance into the community of faith, wherein new self-understanding and faith in the God of Jesus Christ are constantly strengthened and renewed. In such a context transformation and faith do not take place primarily by individual effort and will power.

PREPARING INFANTS AND CHILDREN

In the preparation discussed above, transformation is not only anticipated, but also launched and developed. Consequently, the sacrament of baptism advances, confirms, and strengthens all that already has been taking place. The extensive pastoral work with adults is plain enough from what has been discussed already. It remains now to examine the meaning and practical implications of preparation for the baptism of infants and children in the churches, including the Roman Catholic Church, that provide this means of grace to them. As noted above, in the post-Vatican II era infant and children baptisms are variants on the norm of believers' baptism. The faith that makes infant and children baptisms possible and desirable is that of parents, extended family, and the entire church. The first meaning of preparation, accordingly, is the preparation of this faith. For this reason Frank Dunn suggests, "Preparation for baptism begins ideally with conception."[18] He advocates at least three prebirth meetings with family and

18. Frank Dunn, *Building Faith in Families* (Wilton, Conn.: Morehouse-Barlow, 1986), 80.

sponsors so that a supportive community is formed by the time of birth. Certainly this is a step in the right direction. Before children are born the parents and other family members project images onto them—images of what they will be like, how they will take on the mantle of a hero or victim in the family's past, how they will fulfill the fallen dreams of yesteryear. Children are the focus of parents' love. No doubt part of this love is narcissistic, and ideal images of the self are cast onto the child. Without being aware of it, one sees oneself in the child. Preparation for infant baptism is in fact an encounter with the depths of the human psyche and with the force of the "invisible loyalties" of family generations. Adults' operational faith and their private, family, and cultural myths can be challenged and enlightened by a rehearing of the gospel at this important hour, the beginning of the human life cycle.

Likewise, the preparation of family faith in connection with the birth of a child and his or her baptism is also the time for preparation of the community's faith. Especially before Easter and at other major celebrations in the church year when baptisms are likely to be held, a focus on baptismal faith can renew the life of the community.

In comparison to adult baptism, however, the baptism of infants and children poses a problem. Although the faith of the family and community can be nourished as preparation for baptism, the faith of the infants and children cannot yet be shaped into the conscious, intentional commitment that marks adult baptism. What, then, about the preparation of the faith of these persons for its decisive expression? In some churches, confirmation and first Eucharist immediately follow baptism, regardless of age. In other churches, especially in the West and including the Roman Catholic Church, confirmation and first Eucharist occur after the individual's faith has been nurtured and after self-conscious, intentional commitment to the faith is professed. In these latter churches the gap between baptism and confirmation is a time of preparation. From an adult viewpoint this preparation is dislocated in the sense that it follows baptism, yet confirmation and first Eucharist mark the fulfillment of the conversion envisioned in baptism. Gerhard Podhrodsky's view is representative of Roman Catholic thinking:

> At infant baptism the catechumen rites could well be omitted—but the meaning could be restored to them if, in their place, the various stages of religious education during childhood and adolescence which have replaced the catechumenate (for example, first communion, confirmation, the beginning of a career or of higher education) could all have their own appropriate form of the renewal of baptismal vows.[19]

19. *New Dictionary of the Liturgy,* s.v. "baptism."

In the churches that have confirmation and Eucharist along with infant baptism, childhood growth is simply part of the maturing in faith—or the "divinization"—that has baptism as its foundation. Dynamic psychology has shown that childhood is as much a time of inner and interpersonal conflict as is adulthood, so in principle (although not in specifics) the dynamics of childhood as preparation do not differ from the preparation of adults for the faith that belongs with sacramental life. This means that the church's preparation of children cannot be confined to classroom work and to knowledge acquisition. The calling of the church is to prepare children by addressing their conflicts, standing by them in these conflicts, attending to them, accepting their faults, and recognizing and evoking faith in God through Christ in the power of the Spirit. The church must present the God of Jesus Christ with such force that children's primal images of God and of self are addressed and available for transformation. Accordingly, the pastoral care of children should have the same kind of dimensions as the preparation of adults for baptism: liturgical, communal, mission-related, and educational.

THE RENEWAL OF BAPTISM

The renewal of baptism usually is an annual celebration at the Easter Vigil, and hopefully in most congregations it is part of the celebration of baptisms when they do not take place at Easter. The Presbyterian Church (U.S.A.) and the Cumberland Presbyterian Church in particular have given attention to the possibilities for the renewal of baptism in pastoral care ministry. Their Office of Worship envisions many occasions for such renewal in addition to the Easter Vigil. Referring to early practices in the life of the church, the authors of the document summarize as follows:

> Though baptism could be conferred only once, anointing with oil could be repeated again and again. Each time it brought believers in touch with the grace given in their baptisms and reminded them of the promises made. As such it was a renewal of baptism which the church encouraged its members to receive on many occasions: as preparation to receive the Lord's Supper, especially on the evening of great feasts such as Easter and Christmas; as a form of pastoral care for those who were troubled; and, above all, as part of the church's ministry to the sick and the dying.[20]

Given this association of anointing with baptism, the document provides various services of the renewal of baptism for different situations, public and private. These include the first public profession of faith, renewal for

20. Office of Worship for the Presbyterian Church (U.S.A.) and the Cumberland Presbyterian Church, *Holy Baptism and Services for the Renewal of Baptism: The Worship of God*, Supplemental Liturgical Resource 2 (Philadelphia: Westminster Press, 1985), 18.

those who have been estranged from the church, renewal of baptism for a congregation, renewal marking occasions of personal growth in faith, renewal of baptism for the sick and the dying, renewal of baptism in pastoral counseling, and the reception of members by transfer.

Let us examine one of these services, the Renewal of Baptism Marking Occasions of Growth in Faith. An introductory note explains, "This service may be used in a variety of situations, such as when an individual experiences a significant deepening of commitment or answers the call to a particular ministry in the church. The service may be either private or in the context of corporate worship."[21] The minister reads one or more Scripture passages, then introduces the celebration with words about discipleship and the purpose of the celebration. The minister says to the persons renewing their baptism:

The grace bestowed on you in baptism
is sufficient because it is God's grace.
By God's grace we are saved,
and enabled to grow in the faith,
and to commit our lives in ways which please God.
I invite you now to claim that grace given you in baptism
by renewing your baptismal vows,
to renounce all that opposes God and God's kingdom
and to affirm the faith of the holy catholic church.[22]

Then the persons renounce evil and sin and affirm faith in Christ and the intent to be disciples. The confession of faith (creed) follows, said by all. The minister prays for God's strength and guidance for those renewing baptism, then blesses while laying hands on each. The minister may mark the sign of the cross on the forehead with oil, saying,

_____, you are a disciple of Jesus Christ.
Walk in love, as Christ loved us
and gave himself for us.
Rejoice always, pray constantly,
give thanks in all circumstances;
for this is the will of God in Christ Jesus for you.[23]

The peace concludes the celebration.

This service enables renewal of baptism and strengthening of faith at transitional times in the life story of Christians. It can be used at virtually any transition in the life cycle, and so has great versatility. It can fill many

21. Ibid., 86.
22. Ibid., 88.
23. Ibid., 91.

a gap in the ritual life of the church, especially in the absence of a ritual specifically for the celebration of vocation other than that of minister of word and sacrament.

The great strength of such a renewal service may be its weakness as well. Given that there is no precedent in Scripture for discrete renewals of baptism, one may ask for the justification of a widespread use of such a ritual. Can one kind of liturgy adequately convey divine grace and facilitate the worship of God in so many diverse human transitions? Because it can be applied to various circumstances, the baptismal renewal ceremonies maintain a generality and distance from the pastoral situation. The parallel service for the Renewal of Baptism for the Sick and the Dying, for example, contains no reference to illness, healing, or death. This limitation has been alleviated with the publication of *Services for Occasions of Pastoral Care: The Worship of God* in 1990, which contains liturgies specifically designed for a variety of pastoral care situations.[24]

Another issue raised by the Presbyterian renewal of baptism services has to do with the relation of corporate and private forms of the same ritual. The Presbyterian tradition has forcefully maintained the importance of baptism as a corporate event. Only extreme situations allow for private baptisms, and even then as many representatives of the community of faith as possible are to be present. But in some of the renewal of baptism services, note is made that they may be either public or private without even a preference stated. Should not a tradition known for its emphasis on the corporate nature of baptism avoid the privatization of remembering and renewing baptism? Certainly no great problem arises as long as the actual practice of baptism maintains its corporate setting and integrity. One grants also that pastoral counseling may address personal turning points that should not be made public. The renewal of baptism in pastoral counseling is a private celebration. Still, the question remains: Do the services of renewal of baptism promote an overextension of this pastoral ministry? Surely one can call for limits without denigrating the significance of renewing baptism.

This issue in relation to the renewal of baptism has its parallel in relation to the administration of baptism itself. In some churches, baptism has become a private ceremony, divorced from public worship or the paschal season of the liturgical year. Vatican II's revisions and other attempts at liturgical renewal call for the return of baptism to the corporate setting. But does restoring it to public worship threaten to erode its significance

24. The Ministry Unit on Theology and Worship for the Presbyterian Church (U.S.A.) and the Cumberland Presbyterian Church, *Services for Occasions of Pastoral Care: The Worship of God;* Supplemental Liturgical Resource 6 (Louisville, Ky.: Westminster/John Knox Press, 1990).

as a pastoral care and family celebration? Certainly not, if the various dimensions called for in the structure analyzed above are effectively carried out.

With respect to the renewal of baptism, a general but tentative conclusion in light of the above discussion is this: The renewal of baptism is valid and meaningful annually as part of the Easter Vigil; further, it is valid and meaningful occasionally when affirmation of identity and mission promises to strengthen baptismal faith at crucial junctures in the human life cycle and when no other more specific and appropriate liturgy is available. In my opinion, a strong preference should be given to the public celebration of baptismal renewal.

The question, raised initially at the beginning of this chapter, persists: Can the renewal of baptism be the occasion of a living and transforming memory? My examination of the entire process for the rites of adult initiation in the Roman Catholic Church highlighted that the dynamics of transformation cover preparation and follow-through as much as ritual events themselves. Those dynamics determine whether renewal of baptism becomes an effective source of transformation in churches and personal lives or becomes only an interesting ritual or a sentimental moment for rehearsing what took place in infancy. Genuine renewal of baptism, then, requires cognitive, emotional, ritual, communal, and ethical preparation. The Lenten season and the preparation of persons for their baptism help provide such elements for the renewal of baptism at the Easter Vigil, but pastors need to give further attention to these elements in their pastoral care of individuals who request a ceremony of baptismal renewal. Whether such renewal truly contributes to ongoing transformation in everyday life as well as in worship depends significantly on the concrete reflection and dialogue needed to facilitate new growth and direction in the Christian life.

BAPTISM AND MARRIAGE PREPARATION

In order to think creatively about baptism as the ritual foundation of pastoral care, it is necessary to go beyond thinking about occasions for the renewal of baptism in congregational and individual life. The question is: How can all pastoral care be related to this foundation? The answer cannot be demonstrated here by a detailed review of the various moments of pastoral care and counseling, a review that would endeavor to show how baptism shapes and can reshape such ministries. But one type of pastoral situation can be examined briefly in order to suggest the potential inherent in baptism as foundational for pastoral ministry and counseling.

One area of pastoral care that has become more and more troubling for clergy is marriage. Pastors speak frequently about their frustration with marriage preparation. More and more have come to believe that such preparation is a waste of time because the couples presenting themselves for marriage already are living a romantic illusion that will not bear examination until the realities of married life have commenced. Accordingly, a few pastors have begun to place emphasis on pastoral care as follow-up to weddings. Even though there has been widespread questioning about premarital counseling, some creative efforts have emerged in the life of the church: for example, marriage encounter retreats and training programs; and programs involving sponsoring couples who support an engaged couple, informally discuss their own marital experience with the couple, and model such values as caring but open communication. Can a consideration of baptism yield any concrete contributions toward establishing a more faithful practice of ministry in relation to Christian marriage?

In working with a couple, ministers now habitually ask: Will this marriage last? Given the Christian value of lifelong commitment, that is a relevant question, but it is not the only one. In light of baptism, an equally vital question is: In what way is this marriage transformational?

If marriage is in its essence meant to be transformational, then one might think of the structure for this transformation as similar to that of baptism—that is, a dying to a former way in order to live a new life. In simple terms, such a structure has a period of preparation, the event of marriage, and a follow-up period for consolidating and strengthening the change that has occurred or at least has begun.

With respect to preparation, one might ask whether marriage preparation as I have sketched it is adequate for genuine transformation in light of the model of preparation in baptism reviewed above. How well thought through, enacted, and facilitated are the communal, cognitive, ritual, and ethical dimensions of marriage preparation? Sponsoring couples and the group process entailed in marriage encounter and its offshoots have introduced a communal element. The cognitive element is retained and probably strengthened in these new programs; however, it is important to systematically explore the development of new behavior patterns and attitudes essential to a truly Christian marriage characterized by mutual care and by a mission partnership in the world beyond the marital relationship as such.

The major ritual aspect that has been introduced has been a service of Eucharist at the end of encounter weekends. Although this may be appropriate, much more could be done to strengthen marriage preparation. Preparation for marriage is rightly named a time of "engagement." The process of becoming truly engaged with one another is in dynamic tension with a process of disengagement. With first-time marriages, the disengagement typically is from family of origin so that the process of transformation is marked by a new commitment. In other marriages, the disengagement may be from a former spouse. In any case, the dynamics of engagement-disengagement reverberate deeply in the heart and life of each partner preparing for marriage. One pastor tells of the end of a wedding ceremony that progressed as follows: The couple joined hands; the pastor wrapped his stole around their hands and declared their union; and the bride bolted back to the pew to join her father. The pastor then had to bring her back to the groom and tried to help her to stand in this new place at her husband's side. Certainly, the liturgy and its symbolic action touched her life and revealed to her the significance of what she was doing, but she was unprepared. Is it fair to expect all persons to be prepared for such a transition and transformation? If symbolic action was effective in disclosing her situation to her, then would it not have been wise to have such symbolic action be part of an advance preparation so that the realities of transformation could be appreciated and assimilated over time?

By way of comparison, if preparation for adult baptism entails repeated exorcisms, and if baptism calls for a threefold renunciation of evil, perhaps marriage preparation should involve something like three rites of separation/disengagement! Of course, loyalty to family of origin is not an evil, but it can become an evil when it intrudes on the marriage commitment. Such ceremonies should involve the parents so that they too can be prepared. Suppose that at the beginning of engagement and as a kind of public recognition of the engagement, a ceremony were to occur that would depict and help make concrete the transformation to take place in marriage. It might make a difference in the way a bride-to-be and her mother related and made decisions about wedding arrangements.

The baptismal model also suggests that pastoral care following a marriage could have ritual dimensions. The model should not be applied too literally, for such follow-up is likely to be longer than the *mystagogia* that follows adult baptism. Also, pastoral care that is built on a baptismal foundation combines and balances all the dimensions that make it a means of grace. The revisions or additions here do not imply that ritual as such can take the place of dynamic conversation in pastoral care. Rather, the power in such ministry resides in the interaction of these dimensions as they allow space for the action of God in human life.

Baptism is the liturgical foundation of pastoral care. The new life received grows under the tutelage and shepherding of Christ. Faith in Christ, dying and rising in Christ, and the washing away of sin—which are established realities in Christians' lives through baptism—are to be re-experienced daily in the lives of all Christians, including those entrusted with pastoral care. Thus baptism supports and elucidates the moment-by-moment dynamics of all pastoral care. The dynamics of human transformation are not limited to adult experiences, but pervade all ages through the power of God's presence. Baptism is the initial focus and paradigm for the process of transformation that God is bringing about in Christians' common fellowship and personal living. Accordingly, baptism, including preparation and aftermath, is paradigmatic for all aspects of pastoral care.

CHAPTER 6

The Eucharist: The Eschatological Horizon

Two hospital chaplains are talking over lunch in the hospital cafeteria. One remarks, "Yesterday, a woman called up and wanted me to take Communion to her son, who is here. She said she knew it would help. I went by to see the young man, about eighteen, I should say, and got acquainted. To my surprise he not only was interested in receiving the sacrament but definitely believed that it would 'help.' I just saw him this morning again, and he said that he was feeling better. Now isn't that amazing? What will they say if tomorrow he is feeling worse?"

What understanding of ministry marks this chaplain's self-understanding? What is his view of the sacrament? The impression these few comments leave is that ministry is responding to persons' requests as long as one can maintain some semblance of integrity, even although that may entail an analytical differentiation of one's own beliefs from the perceived beliefs of those to whom one ministers. Obviously the chaplain did not object to administering the sacrament, as long as the patient freely wanted this ministry. Yet the chaplain was amazed that the patient and his mother expected some form of concrete "help" from the sacrament. In fact, the chaplain was so taken with the definiteness of the expectation that he did not pursue the possible meanings veiled in the vagueness of the mother and the son's term "help." It could mean many things, and we have no idea what it meant to them. The term could have referred to improving the young man's physical condition in conjunction with the methods of modern medicine. It could have referred simply to a boost in morale in a time of adversity. The "help" might have been the young man's becoming more aware of the presence and sustaining love of God. The patient and his mother seem to understand the sacrament as a "means," but to what? To some form of grace?

As for the chaplain, perhaps he simply did not have the time to explore the meanings. Alternatively, perhaps he had no particular reason or need to explore this question. If ministry is primarily being supportive to human beings in a time of vulnerability, there is no particular point in discovering the meaning and significance of this request. As long as there is no impediment to providing the hoped-for symbols of support, whether the sacrament or a hand on the shoulder, one should be responsive.

The chaplain's amazement, however, suggests that he detected some expectation that probably transcended vague support, although the persons presenting their need were not theologically articulate. His being impressed with their attitude, whatever it was explicitly, ought to raise a question about his own beliefs and expectations concerning this sacrament. I cannot address this question with respect to this particular chaplain, but the question is a vital one for all pastors and chaplains. Their basic attitudes and beliefs, which are more complex than merely what they consciously profess, determine how they approach this particular moment in pastoral ministry, and all this, I believe, is communicated in the dynamics of actual sacramental ministry.

Theological Expectations of the Sacrament

"Thoroughly modern" ministers, for example—whether conservative or liberal, Baptist or Episcopalian—are likely to have little or no expectation concerning this ordinance or sacrament. For them, rituals and symbols do not have any inherent power or "virtue." They can, of course, serve as graphic aids to the sermonic moment or as expressions of human caring and acceptance, which these ministers believe God does use. But as an aspect of such a scenario or ministry, the Eucharist has at best a supplementary or tangential role.

To approach questions of expectations regarding the Eucharist or the Lord's Supper, I shall examine and analyze an ecumenical text of the sacrament or ordinance. How does the liturgy itself address the question of what expectations can be directed to the Eucharist? What image of God does the liturgy set forth? What are the implications of this sacrament and this vision of God for pastoral care ministry beyond corporate worship?

Answers to these questions will be probed by way of an analysis and reflection on how the text treats the Eucharist as the eschatological horizon of pastoral care. The Eucharist, I shall argue, sets present Christian living in the framework of this horizon of the imminent end that God promises.

Accordingly, the Eucharist is the eschatological horizon for pastoral care ministry as a particular vocation that gives expression to Christian living. The Eucharist sets forth an eschatological horizon by providing a way of sacramental presence in the midst of the absence of the one who came and who is coming again. This sacramental presence transforms Christians' lives and all that they offer to God so as to make them and their offering acceptable to God.

The ecumenical text that I shall chiefly focus upon is from the Church of South India, which has united Christians from Anglican, Congregational, Methodist, and Presbyterian traditions. Unfortunately, the Church of South India's text uses sexist language, which does not communicate effectively the intended, generic meaning. The text does provide an ecumenical liturgy that balances various New Testament eucharistic passages.

THANK OFFERING
The sacramental segment of the worship service for the Church of South India begins with the peace, which is carried out variously according to local custom. Peace and reconciliation with one another prepare the community for presenting an offering that is acceptable to God. The offerings of the people along with the bread and the wine are brought forward and placed on the table during a lyric or hymn. With all standing, the presbyter prays, "Holy Father, you have opened a new living way for us to come to you through the self-offering of Jesus. We are not worthy to offer gifts to you, but through him we ask you to accept and use us and our gifts for your glory. Amen."[1]

The self-offering of Jesus is presented as the living way from humanity to God. The prayer voices the meaning of the offering: Those present are offering themselves and their gifts to God and hope that because of Jesus Christ God will accept them and their gifts, although they are not worthy. The self-giving of Jesus is presented at the very beginning as the basis for the entire liturgical action.

This is a thank offering, the expression of thanks for the gifts of God that the worshipers have received. They have received the gift of life, the wonders of nature, including grain and grape, and the grace of covenantal relationship with God; and they have received God's loving and merciful gift of God's own self—Jesus Christ, "God of God, Light of Light, very God of very God." In the context of these immeasurable gifts, those

---

1. Quotations are from the 1972 revised edition of *The Book of Common Worship* (New York and London: Oxford University Press) as found in Max Thurian and Geoffrey Wainwright, eds., *Baptism and Eucharist: Ecumenical Convergence in Celebration* (Geneva: World Council of Churches, 1983), 179, 180. Hereafter in the text this liturgy will be referred to as *CSI* (for Church of South India).

assembled give symbols of their thanks to God. Although the gifts entail deprivation and sacrifice, they represent and express the spirit of having been abundantly blessed. Indeed, the spirit of thanks cannot be contained in this prayer at the offering, but is elaborated in the Great Thanksgiving or anaphora to follow.

What do the worshipers offer to God? They offer bread and wine and other gifts that represent the work of their lives. The bread and wine represent their work every bit as much as money does, and even more. In making bread people take God's gift of wheat and transform it into food for daily life. In making wine they take God's gift of grapes and transform them into festive drink to celebrate the gift of life. In presenting the bread and the wine the worshipers acknowledge that they have received gifts and life itself from God, and they proffer to God their own work of transforming these gifts. The gifts summarize what they have done with all that God has given them. The gifts symbolize their lives, their vocations and stewardship. It is no wonder, then, that the prayer asks God to use the people and their gifts, because in and with the gifts they are presenting their very selves.

With this offering the process of transformation already has begun, and this transformation is carried forward in the entire liturgy and the life it portrays. The bread and wine are the results of transformation, and now, although the prayer is not a formal blessing, they are no longer just bread and wine. They are objects in the drama of salvation; they are gifts to the God who has created human beings and who has established a covenant of grace with them.

Although the people's response to this grace has not been adequate, in these gifts they hope for the fulfillment of the mutual unity between them and God to which the covenant witnesses. They acknowledge that they have not been wholly present to God, but with these gifts they offer signs of their presence. It is no wonder that a number of Jesus' parables of the kingdom of God portray an absence between parties who have made an agreement. That is the human situation. The covenant with God is the context for the meaning of Christians' lives, yet they are neither wholly present to God nor wholly aware of God's presence with them. So in this existence characterized by such a fundamental absence, they offer tokens of their desire to be present, just as a person becomes present symbolically to another through a *present,* an object that establishes presence in the midst of absence.

This is an offering, a sacrifice, and so it reflects an exchange between God and human beings: God gives, sacrifices, for humankind. Human beings, in turn, give, sacrifice, for God. Such "exchange" suggests not only mutuality but also distance:

> The very idea of exchange supposes awareness of a distance, which is sometimes identified with a radical indebtedness for existence itself. . . . By means of sacrifice human beings try to bridge this distance. They symbolize the desired union by offering something of which they deprive themselves; they thereby renounce the immediate possession of things in order to reach the Giver of them.[2]

The gifts contribute to a relationship during an absence. The present time comprises a community and individual selves in an interim situation where full presence seems not to be possible.

The life-offering and death of Jesus underscore the sacrificial nature of all offering, a reality that underlies many kinds of human relationships. Sacrifice, one might say, is a model of social relationships. When persons sacrifice in social relationships they do not always expect immediate and exact reciprocity. They do hope that what they offer, however imperfect and partial, will be accepted as is. Likewise, Christians' fundamental hope is that God will accept them as living sacrifices (Rom. 12:1). Because the self is constituted by all of its relations, and not merely by its relation to itself, this divine acceptance is more fundamental than self-acceptance and its subtle moralisms. When Christians pray they present the name of Jesus Christ so that their prayer may be an acceptable offering to God; likewise, in the offering and the Eucharist they present the name and sacrificial act of Jesus Christ that their worship and offering may be acceptable to God.

Is this transformation human beings' own work or that of God? Descriptively one can say that some of it is human beings' own work. They transform the wheat and grape so that they become bread and wine. Yet theologically one discerns that God works this transformation through human beings for their own good. But at a deeper level yet, one can glimpse how God is at work in all human work, transforming it in ways human beings do not anticipate or even intend. Christians give over their work to God and offer or lift it to God because they recognize that God takes their work and works with it in God's own way. All of their work must be surrendered to God if they are to envision what is really happening in their lives. They are part of a larger whole; they play a part in a bigger-than-life drama that they understand only partially. So the offering in this liturgy condenses this dynamic of the human condition into a simple but powerful act. As Gabriel Marcel has said, "To be at work . . . is to be possessed

2. Xavier Léon-Dufour, *Sharing the Eucharistic Bread: The Witness of the New Testament* (Ramsey, N.J.: Paulist Press, 1982), 296.

by the real in such a way that we no longer know exactly whether it is we who are fashioning it or it which fashions us." For him, to work is to animate, and "the power of animating is the power of using to the full, or, to go more deeply, of lending ourselves, that is to say of allowing ourselves to be used to the full, of offering ourselves in some way to those *kairoi,* or lifegiving opportunities, which the being, who is really available (*disponible*), discovers all around him."[3]

The liturgy catches worshipers up into the powerful presence of God because it shows them how their daily lives can and are caught up into God's actions. To offer is to become available, and becoming available animates—God welcomes the symbols of the gift of community and self that are presented. The gifts of the offering communicate to God that the worshipers' community and very selves are available for work, for being animated and being transformed. Rigid self-control and control of others, then, are precisely what offering is not. To the extent that Christians continue to try to control the outcome of all that they do, they refuse to offer community and self and they lose the power of the Spirit, the animation that greets the presentation of community and self. In genuine offering one yields control to God and does so freely and thankfully.

When the people present their offering in corporate worship, they profess and enact this faith. When they reflect on their daily experience they know that their daily lives and work, their "gifts," are taken up by others and they cannot tell what will become of these gifts. People take the way others present themselves and create their own representation of them. When people realize what others have made of them, they may protest that they have been misrepresented or they may gain an insight into themselves that could not be acquired otherwise. Or others take the results of one's work in directions one did not foresee, an outcome that one may or may not appreciate but simply cannot control. So in their offering Christians surrender such control and entrust who they are and their work to God. Let there be no mistake about it—if Christians' present gifts and their very selves as an offering they are presenting them for the glory of God, and this means that they are presenting them for transformation. In the eucharistic offering they discover that God's grain and grape are transformed into the bread and wine presented to God, and are transformed further into God's gift to human beings.

Although set in the context of God's covenant with human beings and an interim time, the bringing of gifts to God in this liturgy implies what might be called an eschatological horizon for pastoral care.

3. Gabriel Marcel, *Homo Viator: Introduction to a Metaphysics of Hope,* trans. Emma Graufurd (New York: Harper and Row, 1962), 179, 180.

MEMORIAL

Following the offertory the presbyter and people say: "Be present, be present, O Jesus, our good High Priest, as you were with your disciples, and make yourself known to us in the breaking of the bread. Amen" (*CSI*). The presence of Jesus is essential for Christians' communion with God. As the resurrected Jesus made himself known to his disciples on the road to Emmaus, so this prayer calls for him to be made known in "the breaking of the bread," a symbol for the whole sacramental event. Then follows the dialogue:

The Lord be with you.
And also with you.
Lift up your hearts:
We lift them up to the Lord.
Let us give thanks to the Lord, our God:
It is right to give him thanks and praise. (*CSI*)

Here it is evident that the presbyter and people serve as priests to one another. The dialogue advances the theme of thanksgiving and thereby leads into the eucharistic prayer. This prayer is an act of praise, and given its probable ancestry in the Jewish *toda,* it may be called a sacrifice of praise.[4] The first eucharistic prayer of the Taizé Community makes this very explicit: "Our Father, God of the universe, fill with thy glory our sacrifice of praise. Bless, perfect and accept this eucharist as the figure of the one and only sacrifice of our Saviour."[5]

The eucharistic prayer is an act of praise by way of memory and proclamation. The people of God recall and proclaim with praise the mighty deeds of God from the beginnings of creation. One assumption is that memory enables action. When God remembers Abraham, for example, God blesses. The Taizé Community's prayer proclaims to God and to the people of God, renewing the covenantal relationship: "Through reciprocal remembrance the original relationship will be, and in fact already is, restored."[6] God is present to human beings as they become present to all that God has done throughout the ages. Accordingly, the Church of South India's prayer proclaims:

It is good and right, always and everywhere to give you thanks, O Lord, Holy Father, Almighty and ever-living God; Through Jesus Christ, your Son, our Lord, for through him, you created all things from the beginning,

4. Léon-Dufour, *Sharing,* 40–44.
5. Cited in Max Thurian and Geoffrey Wainwright, eds. *Baptism and Eucharist: Ecumenical Convergence* (Geneva: World Council of Churches; Grand Rapids: Eerdmans, 1983), 180.
6. Ibid., 103.

and made us men in your own image; through him you redeemed us from the slavery of sin; through him you have sent out your Holy Spirit to make us your own people, the first-fruits of your new creation.

And so we join the angels and the saints in proclaiming your glory as we sing (say):

Holy, Holy, Holy Lord, God of power and might, heaven and earth are full of your glory. Hosanna in the highest. (CSI)

The joining with angels and saints lifts time, this present moment, out of itself. In a way the gathered community represents the larger, spiritual community of all generations and beyond. In the Sanctus the gathered community joins the wider continuous action and way of participating in God's being. With this transcendence of ordinary time all things resound with the praise of God.

The prayer continues with the memorial of Jesus' passion and last meal with the disciples:

Truly holy are you, our Father. In your love for us you gave your Son Jesus Christ to be one of us and to die on the cross for us. By that one perfect sacrifice, he took away the sins of the whole world and commanded us to remember his death until he comes again. So, on the night he was betrayed, he took bread, gave thanks to you, broke it and gave it to his disciples, saying: Take, eat; this is my body given for you; do this in remembrance of me. So also after supper he took the cup, gave thanks to you, gave it to them and said: Drink it, all you, for this is my blood of the new covenant, shed for you and for all men, to forgive sin. Do this, whenever you drink it, in remembrance of me.

Amen. Your death, O Lord, we remember, your resurrection we proclaim, your final coming we await. Christ, to you be glory. (CSI)

This portion of the prayer begins by recalling Jesus' death and command "to remember his death until he comes again." So far as Jesus' command is concerned, one peculiarity calls for reflection: The prayer does not go on to rehearse the hours of suffering on the cross. Rather it makes present the meal Jesus had with his disciples, the meal during which he foretold his passion and set it in the context of God's salvation: "It is noteworthy that the account repeated in cult is not of the saving event which is to be commemorated, but of its prefiguration."[7] The remembrance of Jesus' passion and death is indirect, routed by way of the symbolic event that illumines Jesus' sacrifice. This historical meal interprets Jesus' death and provides a meaning not fully articulated in the Gospels' accounts of the event itself.

The sacramental celebration is clearly both a memorial and an awaiting. Although by means of it worshipers are lifted into the eternal, the sacrament

7. Léon-Dufour, *Sharing*, 111.

is temporal; its termination is foreseen and announced: ". . . until he comes again." Meanwhile, the worship, the people's offering of their community and very selves, takes place in the visual absence of Jesus Christ as the object of faith. Jesus Christ is present sacramentally; Jesus Christ is present by the power of the Holy Spirit in this sacramental event and its gifts of bread and wine. But this way of relating, this manner of knowing God and of knowing oneself, is a mode of existence to be transcended in the time of God's consummation of all things. Thus, this sacrament nourishes the people and their faith, but only until that time that—at least in the divine perspective—is imminent. That such sacramental action will cease does not mean that Jesus Christ's being or authority is temporary. Thus the creed proclaims: "Whose kingdom shall have no end."

BLESSING

This prayer concretely this prayer brings to mind Jesus' meal with his disciples: "On the night he was betrayed, he took bread, gave thanks to you, broke it and gave it to his disciples." At any Jewish meal the basic actions of taking bread, blessing it, breaking it, and distributing it to all present were symbolic actions that constituted a community, establishing a harmony and oneness among those present. The blessing is fundamental for both the bread and the cup: "For a Jew to pronounce a blessing is not simply to say some words, it is an action that allows the very current of divine life to come through. The living God has empowered his creatures to transmit *his* blessing. To bless is to communicate the power of God."[8]

The proclamation of these words of Jesus in word and symbolic action enables Christians to be attuned to a fellowship with God and with one another, and so readies them for partaking of this symbolic meal. Verbal proclamation precedes, accompanies, and follows the sharing and ingestion of this meal. This meal, when Christians partake of Christ's body and blood—which were given for others—distills the essence of all meals that celebrate the unity of the biological and the relational. The worshipers, who "inhabit" their bodies, become organic members of a social body and feast together in communion with the divine. Xavier Léon-Dufour comments, "While baptism has already given form to the 'body of Christ,' the Eucharist is this body's food; when believers express themselves in the eucharistic action they maintain and strengthen their personal union with Christ and become, together, the community that belongs to him forevermore. This is the communal fruit of the Eucharist."[9]

The union and social relation enacted in the meal pertain to the divine-human relationship as well as to the spiritual harmony of the community

8. Ibid., 58.
9. Ibid., 213.

of faith. The people have offered to God their gifts, made from what God has first given them. Their gifts are then blessed and transformed so that now they are offering living symbols of God's own self-giving to humankind. In a sense they offer God to God. Then they turn around and consume what they offer—they incorporate and receive that which they give. How dramatically this enacts and conveys the oneness of the divine and the human! In terms of liturgical reality and psychological space God is both without and within.

The eucharistic prayer continues:

> And so Father, remembering that Jesus, your Son and our Lord, was born and lived among us, suffered and died, rose again and ascended, we, your people, are doing this to remember him as he commanded us until he comes again, and we thank you for reconciling and restoring us to you in him.
>   *O Lord, our God, we give you thanks, we praise you for your glory.*
> (*CSI*)

Jesus' command to remember establishes a memorial. In the first eucharistic prayer of the Taizé Community, the memorial itself is presented as an offering: "All things come of thee, and our only offering is to recall thy gifts and marvellous works."[10] A memorial recalls what God has done in the past so that God will grant the same blessings today.[11] In this particular sacrament the memorial also recalls what God promises to do in the fulfillment of time and God's kingdom so that God will grant in abundant measure a portion of these final blessings in advance, even today, in the power of the Spirit.

SACRIFICE

Let us return to the eucharistic prayer:

> And we humbly ask you Father, to take us and this bread and wine, that we offer to you, and make them your own by your Holy Spirit, so that our breaking of the bread will be a sharing in Christ's body and the cup we bless a sharing in his blood. Join us all together in him. Make us one in faith. Help us to grow up as one body, with Jesus as our head. And let us all together, in the Holy Spirit, bring glory to you, our Father. Amen.
> (*CSI*)

These words speak of God's acceptance as God's taking the people and the bread and wine and "owning" them; it is thus a complete receiving.

10. Cited in Thurian and Wainwright, eds. *Baptism and Eucharist*, 181.
11. Max Thurian, "The Eucharistic Memorial: Sacrifice of Praise and Supplication," in Max Thurian, ed., *Ecumenical Perspectives on Baptism, Eucharist and Ministry* (Geneva: World Council of Churches, 1983), 90–103.

Not only is the truly present Christ taken in as we consume this meal, but just as significantly they are taken up into Christ and into God. In Christ the people's offering is accepted. This is why Max Thurian writes, "The eucharist . . . makes the believer a sacrifice acceptable to the Father by the power of the Spirit."[12] Calvin spoke of Christ as "the altar, upon which we lay our gifts, that whatever we venture to do, we may undertake in him."[13] In the sacrament Christ truly is present to and within believers; in the sacrament they become truly present to and in Christ, and in Christ truly present to and part of one another.

Accordingly, in this sacrament believers become present to the past sacrifice of Christ, and the risen Christ is revealed as present to them. Their joint offering and they themselves are fully accepted and taken up into God, preknowing as it were their future existence in God. That possibility that is imminent from God's perspective because God has promised it in Christ is now imminent for the worshipers as well, for they have sampled its reality together. The reality of this liturgical and spiritual existence both transforms them in worship and transforms their understanding of their everyday selves and the lives they lead. As food and drink produce energy for action, participation in the Eucharist energizes for mission. The sacramental, interim participation in Christ and the glimpse of his and the people's future glory energizes them for and lures them into living and working as mission. They return to daily life a renewed and transformed people called to witness to and take part in God's transforming work. Christian mission is both a commission (Matthew and John) and a co-mission: It is ministry with Christ, in the name of Christ, by the power of Christ's Spirit. This evangelical-ethical dimension of the sacrament is essential to its dynamic. If Christians become open to sacramental reality, they hear a summons and know themselves both as graced and as sent ones. The symbolic action of the sacrament causes them to remember, and remembering causes them to act. The sacrament is a plan for action; it is a pattern of action. This is one reason that intercession for others is an essential dimension of the sacrament. In fact, the sharing of the bread symbolizes the service of one another: "Bread is meant to be shared, especially with the hungry; this sharing is the fundamental characteristic of the righteous."[14] The life of service begins in praise and prayer and ends in prayer and praise; it is continuous with worship and in essence is worship.

This understanding of the Eucharist illumines the meaning of mission in the world of everyday affairs. Mission is not busywork, nor is it being

12. Ibid., 90.
13. John Calvin, *Institutes of the Christian Religion,* ed. John T. McNeill, trans. Ford Lewis Battles (Philadelphia: Westminster, 1960), 17.
14. Léon-Dufour, *Sharing,* 58, 59.

good. Mission is living out of a faith vision, and so it is embodied best in symbolic actions. Worship enables Christians to discern in secular life which actions truly speak, which actions communicate in ways that bless and transform. Liturgy is not ideology, so there is no pat formula for deriving Christian action from the liturgy. Rather, prayerful discernment discovers the ways sacramental action becomes meaningful mission, replete with signs of divine justice and mercy. The sacramental Christ present in Christians corporately and individually moves them to truly and genuinely be present to others, usually a greater service than doing odds and ends for others or ministering "to" them. And when people truly give themselves by their presence and in whatever service they render, they discover how spontaneously and readily others are available to them and minister to them, just by their presence.

Thus praxis that is faithful to faith's renewed visioning of God is the enactment of the eucharistic prayer and comes about only by prayer. Such praxis is the extension of liturgical reality, especially sacramental being, into everyday reality and profane doing, a doing that is not so much duty as it is being. The flowing movement from liturgical to secular living is evident in the eucharistic prayer of the Consultation on Church Union (U.S.A.): "Grant that in praise and thanksgiving we may be a living sacrifice, holy and acceptable in your sight, that our lives may proclaim the mystery of faith. . . . Grant that we may be for the world the body of Christ, redeemed through his blood, serving and reconciling all people to you."[15]

The Eucharist is a means of grace in part because it is a means of a life of service. The Christian life is a movement from death to life (baptism), from life to joy (Eucharist), and from joy to fruit (sacramental living).

Psychological Reflections on Images of Eating

The symbols of eating and sacrifice reinforce the sense of the transitoriness of all things, human beings included. The grain and grapes undergo transition and are changed into bread and wine, and they undergo transition when they are taken up, blessed, distributed, and consumed. By taking part in this drama of transformation, Christians undergo transition, are transformed, and are given over to further transformation.

In psychological terms, one can say that the bread and wine as transitional images induct Christians into the true world of transition. The psychological "space" is described as a "transitional space," which means that it is not just space, certainly not literal space. In this transitional sphere

---

15. Cited in Thurian and Wainwright, *Baptism and Eucharist*, 185.

something occurs—there is a temporal dimension. With reference to the Eucharist, psychological space is constituted by the temporal boundaries of past and future—an interim world foreshadowing its culmination. The "space" is created and constituted by "the times." The past memorialized and the future proclaimed are sacred times that make for a present time that is set apart, sacred, open to the divine, a present moment in sacramental space. As the sanctuary assembles the people and sends them forth, so personal consciousness assimilates this twofold action through participation in the liturgy.

Psychology can describe this space that interrelates subject and object, disclosing a relational whole from which the integrity of self and other derives. But psychology does not fill this space unless it begins to function as a philosophy of self-understanding or as a religion. The contents of this space are filled by culture and religion, grasped by human faith, criticized by reason, and worked out in daily praxis.

In worship a community faith is presented and enacted symbolically. As individuals participate in worship they recapitulate and interpret this faith, making it part of their own psychic being and self-understanding. To a significant degree, however, this living, community faith has its way with them, binding them one to another, moving and repositioning them, and so making possible this personal appropriation and transformation. The space of the personal psyche, then, is filled with the symbolic action, word, and spirit of the community's faith presented in the Eucharist. In actual worship the individual is lifted by aspects of this faith, struggles with some aspects, plays with other aspects, and disregards still others. The faith presented in worship is a special environment for the community and the souls of its members, an environment that engages and draws out the spirit within.

In the Eucharist the fundamental object for faith is God made known and available in Christ through the powerful presentation of the Holy Spirit. This object is not the creation of the individual self. Such worship challenges the idiosyncratic idols of personal believing and offers new life to the individual as part of this loving, believing, and hoping community. In the Church of South India's liturgy God is presented as caring Father, yet as one who is holy, in relation to whom human beings are unworthy. Thus there is a caring spirit, but it is distant. Despite this distance God gives gifts, even the gift of God's own self. If human beings' gifts to God can be made acceptable, then a mutuality and oneness are possible between God and humanity. This possibility and reality are enacted and realized in the Eucharist because in Christ, whom God has given, human beings' gifts and very selves become acceptable to God (Mal. 3:3). In the liturgy God is presented as one who transforms and reconciles. God gives human beings

gifts; God transforms their gifts, making these gifts and the people themselves acceptable; and God transforms human beings, re-creating them as
God's gifts to others and re-creating them through the gifts of others.
Christians affirm that the Holy Spirit permeates liturgical actions and
animates the word proclaimed through these actions and along with them.
The sacrament is not the only locus of the Spirit's transformation, but it
positions the people of God so that they can discern the many cultural,
social, and personal loci of the Spirit's work. The Spirit animates sanctuary,
soul, and street corner so that they become places where God's presence
can be felt and known. The Spirit makes the symbols, words, and sacramental actions numinous so that they point beyond themselves, becoming
vehicles of faith and not primary objects of faith, opening community and
individual to the true subject-object of faith, the God of the crucified and
risen Christ. Thus the Spirit overfills liturgical action so as to burst into
everyday action, and overflows from the marketplace of profane life into
the sanctuary. The Spirit gives God's self and evokes our self-giving to
God and others. In the Spirit the name of Christ is alive in sanctuary and
soul. In the Spirit the presence of Christ is brought to culture and nature.
In Christ human beings and all that they offer to God are accepted and
transformed for the glory of God.

Given these reflections, the following question arises: In what way is
this sacrament a means of grace? Current liturgical discussions, even in
the Roman Catholic tradition, deemphasize this framework for understanding the sacrament. Rather than a means of grace it is to be understood as
a mystery that, although incomprehensible, enlightens the soul. The new
emphasis follows the lead of the Eastern Orthodox tradition on the sacraments. The difficulty being avoided is the traditional Western understanding of causality, according to which the sacrament causes the grace
to which it testifies to "happen." This shift is understandable, given the
wooden and mechanical attitudes that grew out of the traditional view. But
something is lost in this change, something that was alluded to in the young
man's comment recorded at the beginning of this chapter—the comment
that the sacrament "helped." Cannot the sacrament be a vehicle, a means,
and not thereby be the necessary and sufficient cause? Christians can and
should, I think, envision a Spirit who in this interim time works through
concrete events and actions that themselves are not to be worshiped but
do in fact lead human beings into the divine presence and convey the divine
mercy in specific ways, such that Christians can participate in these events
and actions regularly with expectant devotion.

Implications for Pastoral Care

The above analysis and reflections are responses to an ecumenical text
of the eucharistic liturgy, and so are centered on the situation of public

worship. Do the analysis and reflections have implications for pastoral care ministry beyond the corporate situation? What does it mean to think eucharistically about pastoral care with families, small groups, and individuals? How does a sacramental, eschatological context for pastoral care affect what pastoral care and counseling understand themselves to be and do? Do the themes of the Eucharist and the connection between public sacrament and pastoral ministry help pastors and counselors to envision the cultural context and social justice dimension of their ministry?

OFFERING

If Christians are indeed in an eschatological situation of partial fulfillment, symbolic understanding, and transitional action, then their hopes and plans, their thinking and interpretation, their work, play, and worship as Christians are offerings to God. If the Christian life is a life of service offered to God, then the whole of pastoral care ministry is likewise a service offered to God. To the extent that the Eucharist discloses and underscores this truth it is the root from which the central issue, clinical and pastoral, in the Clinical Pastoral Education (C.P.E.) movement has grown: the issue of one's genuine availability as a person to others. C.P.E. can be counted on to raise this issue for its participants. Underlying this issue is the assumption that ministry is honest self-giving, or self-giving that is self-aware. Put simply, it is offering. In being with others, are pastors truly themselves—do they offer their genuine selves? In what they do for others, are they actually forthcoming—do they give of themselves? Along with raising these issues and question, C.P.E. has had the wisdom to discern the essential mutuality involved: As one ministers to others one receives as much or more from them, and one ministers to others by receiving what they give—their "offerings," their being who they are in the moment. In the mutual sharing of selves, however broken, wholeness is discovered.

C.P.E. has been less effective in advancing the principle that ministers' personal availability to others says something fundamental about their availability to God and their freedom to offer themselves, who they are and what they do—to God. Nor has C.P.E. or pastoral counseling, in the United States at least, discerned the significance of worship with sufficient clarity to integrate worship and sacramental life into its training and practice.

I believe that the religious dimension of the issue of personal availability and genuineness is vital. Self-acceptance and acceptance of others do indeed help ready persons to envision the greatness of God's acceptance. The significance of pastors' lives as offerings and the power of God's grace to make their offerings acceptable are richly proclaimed and enacted in the sacrament. How appropriate, then, that in pastors' own lives they observe the sacrament and in their pastoral care ministries readily make it available to others as part of who pastors are and what they can offer. The sacrament discloses the grounds for human beings' mutual acceptance of one another. It conveys as well the force of God's acceptance. The effect is that Christians' self-esteem no longer need be based solely on their own efforts to like themselves or on their aligning themselves with the right people who will accept them at critical times. Sacramental self-esteem is grounded in God's esteem for human beings, which was begun and sustained in their creation, is advanced and sealed in their redemption, and is celebrated in worship and life. Irenaeus of Lyons puts it in this way: "The oblation of the Church, therefore, which the Lord gave instructions to be offered throughout the world, is accounted with God a pure sacrifice, and is acceptable to Him; not that he stands in need of a sacrifice from us, but that he who offers is himself glorified in what he does offer, if his gift is accepted."[16]

BLESSING

Within this framework one can discern the importance of blessing in pastoral care. Pastoral care that is a true offering is pastoral care that blesses, and does so personally, ritually, and verbally. Paul Pruyser has suggested that pastors often fail to bless people because their confidence in divine providence has been undermined. Elaine Ramshaw sees another obstacle: pastors' distaste for hierarchical authority.[17] She believes that the words and actions of blessing derive from divine grace and not the person of the pastor and that such a "word of approbation" should not be withheld.

What is of interest here, however, is not so much the obstacles that may keep pastors from blessing but the positive reasons for doing so. If, as the analysis above has shown, to bless is to communicate the power of God, then the simple act of blessing is a dynamic opportunity for pastoral ministry. The community-creating oneness of the blessing of the elements in the sacrament is extended in pastoral ministry so that pastor and person are brought together by the power of the Spirit. A blessing acknowledges and raises consciousness of God's presence. This presence is elusive, a presence in the midst of absence, and needs to be recalled in concrete ways. In pastoral care the blessing personalizes the celebration of God's presence, just as the rite of reconciliation personalizes the evangelical proclamation of the forgiveness of sins in corporate worship.

Along with prayer, a simple blessing is pastoral ritual in its most informal style, and so it often flows readily with the interpersonal dynamics of pastoral visits and conversations. A blessing can take many forms, from

---

16. Quoted in Thurian, "Eucharist Memorial," 91.
17. Elaine Ramshaw, *Ritual and Pastoral Care* (Philadelphia: Fortress Press, 1987), 59–61.

the blessing of a house, to offering the blessing at a meal in the home, to the simple words "The Lord be with you." One pastor developed a simple ritual whereby at the beginning and end of most pastoral visits he said, "The Lord be with you," and the person or persons responded, "And also with you." Many persons feel blessed just by a pastor's visit, so such a ritual with these simple words strengthens and makes overt what is already experienced. Furthermore, blessing and affirming the person create a context in which confrontation can be less threatening, and so defensiveness is less needed.[18]

COMMUNITY

When the Eucharist is taken to the individual and celebrated beyond the sanctuary, does it become a privatized matter between the individual and God? Just the opposite is the case, and that becomes clear when one examines the dynamics of the whole movement from sanctuary to the homes and institutions of the absent ones. If the blessing in the Eucharist unites the community that has voiced reconciliation and peace to one another, then the Eucharist taken from the sanctuary to the marginalized and vulnerable who cannot attend worship binds them and makes them one with the worshiping community. Here communion with Christ comes sacramentally and it comes through and with the marginalized. They enrich the community of faith as they are reunited with it sacramentally. Certainly these persons are in a position to know about and to remind more active Christians of the Christ of the passion, the one who revealed God in his suffering. Through the sacrament they are made present to the community even though absent. In some churches when the Eucharist is celebrated those who are to receive the sacrament after the service in homes and institutions are included specifically in the prayers of intercession.

I can imagine no more significant ministry than this caring for those whose infirmities isolate them from the community. Yet many pastors have become so habituated to the stimulus and demands of meetings and programs that their neglect of this ministry hardly registers except as the vague but tolerable guilt over an unfinished agenda item. In too many places isolated persons virtually would have to make a formal, written request before it would be deemed important that they participate in the Eucharist. In some instances these neglected ones are the very people who in former years had led the church through crises and contributed substantially to its welfare and witness. There is no better vehicle than the Eucharist for

18. On respect as the moral and dynamic principle linking empathy and confrontation in pastoral care, see Ralph L. Underwood, *Empathy and Confrontation in Pastoral Care* (Philadelphia: Fortress Press, 1985).

reminding all the isolated that they and their prayers are treasured by God and esteemed among the faithful.

The neglect of sacramental ministry among the communally marginalized is not simply the fault of the pressures of bureaucratic busyness in parish life. Many pastors have simply forgotten the theological significance of environment, the way God uses various places and events as means of God's work. These pastors may believe that sanctuaries, symbolic objects, and inspired words are necessary to open people to God, but they may need also to learn how to "make sanctuary" in everyday life. Along with this pastors should acknowledge that their worship is incomplete until they share grace and are graced as they make community with the isolated by concrete contact, presence, and sacramental celebration. When the concrete bonds of community to marginalized persons are no longer treasured, then sacramental ministry with the isolated is neglected.

Absence is a powerful force in the lives of shut-ins. Typically their social world has dwindled to caretakers and perhaps one or two loved ones. It is essential that ministers call on them regularly, making available both their presence and the means of grace; it is also essential that shut-ins have the opportunity to minister regularly to visitors. It is only right that shut-ins be called on regularly and be regularly called thankfully to offer themselves, their prayers, and whatever else they can share. A ministry of presence in the midst of absence is vital even if the social skills of these shut-in persons are virtually gone. They belong to an interim community whose oneness is known by being celebrated sacramentally.

THE CASE OF GEOFFREY AND JOHN

A concrete event of pastoral ministry can illustrate some of these implications and so aid reflection on them. The event is the simple act of administering the sacrament to two hospital patients. It occurs in the life of a United Church of Christ minister whom I shall call Jim. Jim is in his forties and is pastor of a church in a small city with a noted university. His completion of a D.Min. degree has helped revitalize him and his sense of ministry. One aspect of his growth has been a renewed interest in sacramental ministry. Having encountered numerous issues and insights through his contact with ministers and priests of diverse churches in his D.Min. program, he feels that he has much to think through and work out in terms of his understanding of the sacraments and their place in his ministry. At the personal level he is aware that he has tended to emphasize the value of his own preaching and now senses a call to explore the more objective dimensions of ministry, the aspects that are not dependent on his personal gifts, although he does not diminish these talents.

In his hospital visitation, Jim has been visiting a parishioner, Geoffrey, and his roommate, John.

Geoffrey has lived in this university town for over fifty years. Recently his wife died and he lives alone. His only living blood relative is a niece, who lives on the West Coast. She is to visit him as he comes home from surgery, and will stay with him for several weeks. Geoffrey is retired from an electric utility company, which has a very active program for retirees. He visits nineteen fellow retirees each month as part of a volunteer, continuing contact program. Geoffrey serves as an anchor for others, and by being an anchor feels anchored himself, even though he himself is not deeply reflective. His company sponsors four dinners each year for retirees in addition to various tours and social activities.

One notices Geoffrey's eyes right away. They are clear and expressive. He is over six feet tall and has very thin, white hair. Although he is retired, he usually wears a tie and jacket, yet somehow he never looks stiff or formal, not overdressed. He looks as if he still works for his company, but on a part-time, consultative basis. He has an air of unassuming dignity.

Geoffrey's attendance at the United Church of Christ is quite regular. In addition, he attends a men's prayer breakfast that is held twice monthly. He no longer holds a church office, but years ago served as the church treasurer for a significant number of years. He impresses one as being fact-oriented more than possibility-oriented, but he is not a legalist and is not opposed in principle to changes in the life of the church. The pastor, Jim, likes Geoffrey and finds him to be personable and constructive, although not exuberant or creative. Geoffrey possesses a kind of reserve that has not stifled his warmth yet enables him to center his life on things other than intimacy.

Jim conducted the funeral for Geoffrey's wife, Hazel, and has visited with him in his home a couple of times since then. Currently Geoffrey is in the local hospital for a prostatectomy. The pastor brought the sacrament to him on a Sunday afternoon before the surgery and met his roommate John, who asked if he could receive the sacrament also.

John is also scheduled to have a prostatectomy. John has been baptized but has never regularly attended any church. He is seventy-seven years old and has a history of two strokes, but now is sufficiently stable to allow surgery. He has been taking four different medications daily as part of his health maintenance. At home he lives alone. A son stops by daily to check on him and be sure that he is on the proper schedule with his medications. John has two grandsons. His father died of a heart attack at forty, when John was about ten years old. The father had a history of infantile paralysis. John has a sister who is older by three years, and a sister who is nine years younger. The older sister visits him occasionally, but the younger sister, a fervent Baptist, thinks of John as a "bloody heathen" and has not visited him in years. The religious issue widened a gap that already had existed before the sister had married into a devout Baptist family. Some time after the father's death, John had sided with this sister, who was rebellious, against their mother. One argument ended with John striking his mother in the face. The mother did not speak to him for more than five months. Later, John and his sister were to discover that their mother's way of treating them was in part related to a rare disease that she had and they did not know about. John blames the father for not telling them before he died. Apparently, the distance between sister and brother began with the guilt and tragedy both sensed in relation to their mother.

John had youthful ambitions of going to college. He remembers a scholar-hero whose portrait was on a wall at his high school. John planned to go to the university where this scholar taught. Instead, John had to work. Eventually he became an X-ray machine salesman based in the university town where he had hoped to study. His work brought him into contact with a number of the university departments and with a local hospital. He in fact met and became fairly well acquainted with the scholar he had admired as a youth.

John's wife died five years ago of cancer. This was a few years after his mother had died. His wife came through major surgery "with dignity." As death approached she was heavily sedated, and John remarked, "Sad to say, she died, and I was there and didn't even realize it." This remark struck a chord with what he had said earlier about his mother, how she was ill without his even being aware of it.

John is a talker and is in no hurry to quit. He launches into a conversation without hesitation and will dominate if others are at all passive. It is as if by being absorbed in the telling of his own tale, he lacks a keen sense of others and of the nuances of give-and-take in a conversation. Even so, although he may wander a bit, he is coherent and has good progression of thought with a responsive listener. He has slight difficulty speaking clearly and has to work at making his speech correlate with his thoughts. He complains that he cannot write in longhand, but he can do limited typing on "my wife's typewriter." He lives in the same house where he and his wife lived for many years. When he speaks, he maintains good eye contact. One eye is bloodshot. He is responsive to humor but does not interject a sense of the comic into a conversation.

The pastor, Jim, noticed how John became philosophical when he speaks about war and about nature programs he has seen on TV that recount the cruelty of animals, including parental aggression toward offspring. He views hatred and love in human affairs as "interlocked" in such a way that no one can know truly what to make of them. He says that except for advances in medical technology he would have died long ago, but he hopes to remain independent until "they" take him out of his home "feet first."

John's self-image contrasts with that of his parents, especially his father, who was sickly and did not enjoy longevity. He seems to pay no more attention to his own illness than is necessary. He mentions that some "society" has helped him to deal with the unanswerable questions that religion raises, but remarks quickly, "But that is another story." Whatever the identity of this society, he believes that Christianity makes more sense than other religions.

John has few strong impressions or images of his parents. No doubt he felt abandoned at his father's death, and perhaps abandonment is an enduring theme that began much earlier, even in his infancy. Probably his early representation of God, based on his parental images, was not strong. In his youth and early adulthood he found a substitute father figure and reworked his image of God so that reason and order predominated. Vocationally he found a way to contribute to the welfare of the sick, but at a distance. It is evident that hostility between generations is a theme unresolved still.

During their few days together Geoffrey and John have formed an unlikely alliance. Geoffrey provides a quiet, calming dignity for John, which seems to help the vagabond in John to control himself. When John says something outrageous but Geoffrey refuses to blink, John's inner storm subsides. Just as Geoffrey provides esteem and order, John helps to free Geoffrey by saying things, sometimes both reflective and outrageous, that Geoffrey does not say but wishes he had. Their conversations stretch for the high and the earthy in God and envision them together.

Now, on a quiet Sunday afternoon, these two are about to partake of the Eucharist together with Geoffrey's pastor, Jim. At Jim's arrival, they greet one another, talk briefly about the events of the day, and take time to get better acquainted. On the window stands a pot of Easter lilies, which John's son had brought. It is a bright spring day, and the room is bright and warm and seems larger than it really is. Jim is aware of a sense of harmony and readiness. He makes a couple of remarks about the corporate service of worship, mentions the names of several persons for whom the congregation is praying, asking Geoffrey and John both to contribute their prayers. He does this in a manner that includes John as well as Geoffrey. He briefs both men on what to expect in the celebration of the sacrament, so that they can participate readily. Although the service is a much-shortened version of the Sunday morning Eucharist in the sanctuary, Jim does include the passages for the day: Psalms 121 and 126; Ezra 3; and Revelation 3:1-13. Also, he comments on them briefly and observes a few moments of silent meditation so that the Scriptures are given time to speak. Psalm 121 speaks in a very personal voice, while Psalm 126 has a more corporate emphasis, and Jim comments on the balance of personal and community faith. He lifts up the themes of repentance and steadfastness from Revelation 3, and the joy of restoration from Ezra. A time of silence follows the receiving of the Communion elements, and then Jim says a concluding prayer and benediction.

It was all very simple, and yet Jim felt moved in this event and believed that Geoffrey and John were moved as well, for they seemed to give themselves over to the celebration. As they said their good-byes, Jim noticed how spontaneous Geoffrey was, his eyes dancing as John sat there with a knowing smile on his face.

Driving out of the parking lot, Jim began to reflect on the experience. The three men had not paused to discuss and analyze with one another what this event meant to them, but the thought came to Jim that John's receiving of the Eucharist for the first time in a long while was a kind of restoration for John and for the whole church. John's participation was not a matter of being polite or even friendly. He wanted very much to take part and seemed less isolated than when Jim first met him. He seemed to feel at home without any need to move himself onto conversational center stage. A phrase came to Jim, one he had not thought of for years. It was Anton Boisen's "fellowship of the best." Boisen used it to describe his own inner healing and reconciliation to a sense of community and acceptance with the people who represented God's love to him. And then Jim associated the theme of repentance with Geoffrey. If only for a moment, he seemed free and possessed of a poetic rather than prosaic mentality.

Jim felt that the theme of steadfastness was salient. How often had he wearied under the demands of his work? How often had his own faith and love grown dull as each week made almost everything become increasingly familiar. But now he felt these two men had renewed and readied him to go on and endure and even grow. They had given him their vitality and put him back in touch with his own. Jim chuckled at the thought that often his automobile was more of a sanctuary where God seemed to be with him and to speak than was the church building where he pastored. He knew that the inspiration of this moment would pass, that he and his faith were incomplete, and so it was with John and Geoffrey; yet he was extremely thankful for this day and the light of God's presence. It did not seem that he had given more of himself than usual in this pastoral visit, but he had noticed that something special had been emerging in Geoffrey and John's relationship, and he had been fascinated by it. Certainly, he believed that a mutual ministry had taken place, and that God was present with them in Christ. He was aware of having been blessed by these persons, and wished that he had voiced this feeling or had initiated a ritual blessing at the close of the visit. Perhaps, Jim thought, he should have solicited some verbal reflections on the event for them to look at together before he left.

Then he might know whether he was getting fanciful just now. Still, to do so might have spoiled the moment by imposing too quickly the task of articulation on the wonder of God's grace in action. He decided that he would be alert to an opportunity for some reflection with Geoffrey and John on a follow-up visit, yet he realized immediately that it was more important to trust God and offer up the ministry without collecting explanations.

Jim thought of God as in some sense being always present, yet also as coming and going. Jim could call on God at any time, and usually a sense of God's presence would come, but in an unpredictable way and moment. The only problem seemed to be that Jim did not call on God more often. These were not new thoughts, but Jim was left wondering if God was not laying groundwork for a richer knowing and love for God. John, of course, was a new wonder for Jim. The major clue to personal transformation was Jim's awareness of newness in Geoffrey—certainly his image of Geoffrey was changing, and new images of others imply the formation of new understandings of God and self. Grateful for this visit with Geoffrey and John and the sharing of the sacrament together, Jim appreciated more fully that a sense of God's presence in Christ in the sacrament, whatever the setting, is always related to the community of persons—past, present, and in a sense future as well—made present to one another through the grace of God.

This pastoral event shows how one pastor entered into his ministry with a parishioner and his hospital roommate. It was a sacramental ministry in the literal sense, and eucharistic themes stimulated some reflection on the pastor's part. The sense of aliveness that emerged in this ministry may have been quite transient, but even so it prefigures the future hope that faith presents to us. In fact, the vitality and wonder encountered here came at a period of personal and professional growth, and so may reappear more frequently in diverse dimensions of Jim's ministry. The complementarity and oneness discovered and initially explored in Geoffrey and John's relationship may also have been quite transient, but even if so those characteristics are no less precious or prophetic. Nor do we know whether or not this ministry led to John's return to active and regular participation in the life of some church and the sacrament. But it is not too much to believe that God was at work in this sacramental event and even to hope that the mental images of God and self in all participants were in the process of being transformed. In any case, these fragmented lives were touched by the wholeness that God gives and so the men have much to be thankful for and much to offer one another and God, although their lives are far from complete. The sacrament renders a truth: The promised future is not yet present in fullness, but these lives are spoken for.

A case study cannot illustrate all the implications discussed in this chapter. Nor does the kind of analysis proffered here resolve the many theological issues about the divine presence in the sacrament. Still, the case study and the above discussion elucidate the vital potential of sacramental ministry, especially eucharistic ministry.

Such ministry is part of a universal ministry that has social and cultural as well as personal dimensions. Of necessity, the emphasis here has been on the personal, and it is essential that in all pastoral care the individual not be neglected.

THE EUCHARIST AND A DREAM

The following illustration will extend the Eucharist by applying it to a text different from a case study. Another minister, Dale, is somewhat older than Jim in the above case. Dale had a dream that communicates some of his self-understanding and understanding of ministry. The following is his account of the dream:

> In my dream I suddenly have an urge to ask for special donations for a colleague's church. I do not like fund-raising and I pass such things on to others as much as I can. In this dream, however, I am moved to ask for a contribution from an elderly woman, Lenora. In reality she is a woman in my parish who died recently. In the dream she is dressed in black and is stooped, as she was in life. Yet she is different—she has a sense of purpose and strength. She is not preoccupied with herself. She has come to terms with her destiny. It seems she had been waiting for me to visit. I recall bits of several visits, each one orchestrated so that future generations were present. In one visit, we talked about the right kind of giving when her young cousin was present. In another visit my own daughter was there as she was when she was a child. It seemed important that an example of consultation and of giving was being modeled for them.
>
> In another segment of this dream, I am confronted by the cousin, who now is an adult. He exerts power in the life of the parish and is using his influence to remove the present pastor of the church, whom he sees as being too informal and too interested in unsuitable people. The cousin tells me of the importance of winning and I hear myself reply, "If I win I hope not to notice." A part of me that is observing this dream realizes that I have won the interchange. I want to forget the sensation of winning in loyalty to the ideal of not noticing.
>
> In another part of the dream I am in a tower of a castle and I see children of all kinds, boys and girls of different ages, entering the tower with glee. They flood the tower, virtually empty a minute ago, and they are climbing. I realize that the cousin, without saying a word, has allowed them to enter.

This dream reflects movement in the psychic life of this minister. The primary task, however, is not to interpret all the psychodynamics, but to relate the themes delineated above from the eucharistic liturgy to this dream; that is, to let the images and power of the eucharistic liturgy encounter the images of the dream. The assumption is that while the dream is not about the Eucharist, the sacrament's meaning and power move through all of life. The private nature of the dream cannot be subsumed into the public testimony of the liturgy, yet the liturgy can put questions to the dream and suggest possible directions of meaning. The eucharistic text can help uncover the eschatological dimension of the dream.

The theme of offering is overt in the dream. Perhaps regular participation in the Eucharist as an exercise of faith in Christ helps to educe dreams like this. In the interchange with the woman, the conversation itself as well as the example of planned generosity are offered to future generations. In the next portion of that dream the well-laid plans of the first portion seem to have been undone or forgotten. The cousin has become a person committed to values of winning and propriety. The cousin represents Dale's alter ego, a part of him he tends to disown but can recognize, and the dream conveys a new readiness to confront this part of himself. The cousin also represents powerful cultural forces that endeavor to maintain their own preferred order and exclude the poor and the childlike. Does the dream call this pastor to engage and address these forces in his ministry? Does the dream call him to lead the people in his charge to do likewise?

Another dimension of the image of offering may be derived from the symbol of the castle tower. The tower seems to say to him, "I am wondrous when you see me with children's eyes. I am the secret place. I am solitude, your strength. You are to share your strength with others, to help others discover the secret strength of solitude." Is not this pastor being called to offer more of himself to others?

In contrast to the ubiquitous theme of offering, the theme of memorial is not overt in this dream. One had best not read it into the dream, although a definite element of time is apparent in the dream. Lenora who has died still lives in the dream. Strengths not readily seen in her now shine forth. The dream may challenge Dale's tendencies to neither recognize women's actual and latent strengths nor accept his own shadow side. When reflecting on his dream Dale imagined a dialogue with Lenora, and part of what she said to him was, "I want you to know that everyone has strengths, something to give; I want you to understand people now in light of their final strength, the moment of their destiny."

The fluctuation of time exists in the dream; Dale's daughter, an adult, lives in the dream as a child. In the first portion of the dream she and the cousin also represent the future as do the children in the tower. Psychodynamically, Christ is memorialized in dreams in the form of one's ego ideal. Dale's ego ideal is evident in the dream as the one who models conversation and giving, and as the one who confronts forces of domination. The dream distills elements of community: the partnership of Dale and Lenora; the dialogue of conflicting perspectives in the interchange between the cousin and Dale; the inclusion of children who had been excluded. The feeling of community puts Dale in touch with a deep desire and provides concrete scenarios that represent the direction and scope of his desire. In the dream's vision of community, others are depicted in different ways. The feminine is presented as experienced, abundant, wealthy, and wise. The masculine other is envisioned as one who is complex: exposed to generosity and cooperation in the past, able to rethink a position in the present, and able to act out of a transformed self-understanding.

Giving attention to the eschatological dimension of the dream allows one to envision Dale's story in light of Christ's story. In this reading of the dream the forces that create it are submitted to a horizon of possible meanings and to time that is imminent and exaggerates in the direction of the truth. It is appropriate, therefore, that Dale accept the dream as a blessing and present the dream itself and its interpretation to God as an offering. Reading the dream in light of the Eucharist enhances the larger vision in the dream and helps Dale to appropriate the dream's meanings for his life and ministry.

In and through faith Christians proclaim and celebrate the presence of Christ in their midst. This presence is known in the eucharistic celebration and in the elements of bread and wine. Such knowledge is a sacramental knowing, an interim knowing that, with each celebration, reestablishes a transitional way of being for the community and for individual participants. Community and self are given over, offered, and, although fragmented and unworthy, transformed and made acceptable. In the sacramental actions individuals yield themselves to actions that are not merely their own doing, actions that undo and redo their lives and relationships, transforming their very being as well as energizing and directing their becoming.

Ours is an interim situation. In this situation pastoral care helps to provide a facilitating environment in which people can wait for God, who in Christ has already come and is yet to come. In pastoral ministry the community celebrates the elusive and divine presence made known through absence and celebrated sacramentally. Through representative members this faith community reaches out to remind the isolated and marginalized of their belonging, waits for God with them sacramentally, and offers gifts and selves in Christ, trusting in God's transforming of the gifts and of the waiting. Remembering Christ's death, celebrating his resurrection, and awaiting his imminent return animate pastoral care.

Perhaps it is inevitable, at least it is appropriate, that my initial reflection on the divine presence and absence in relation to prayer now comes full circle, reconsidered in relation to the Eucharist. Located where the eschatological horizon can be glimpsed, one can appreciate that pastoral care is a ministry of symbolic communication, a ministry of word and sacrament in dialogue with silence.

Conclusion: Freedom, Order, and Transcendence

The preceding chapters have analyzed some of the basic means of grace in the Christian tradition: namely, prayer, divine reading (*lectio divina*), reconciliation, baptism, and Eucharist. The analysis has been both theological and psychological. Where specific texts for worship have been discussed, they have been interpreted with an ecumenical audience in mind, and they have been read for their implications for pastoral ministry beyond the public sanctuary. The aim throughout has been to demonstrate and support a thesis, one that emphasizes the essential place of ritual in pastoral care ministry. In particular, the argument has been that renewal in pastoral care today depends on a reappropriation of religious resources, means of grace, in a manner that balances freedom, order, and transcendence. The assumption is that a community's common life of worship is the key source of energy, guidance, and inspiration for pastoral care when it effectively communicates divine grace in human lives.

Prayer as the Soul

At the very core of pastoral care is the spirit of prayer. Deep caring and the spirit of prayer are closely linked, and where there is the spirit of prayer there is grace. Thus prayerfulness is essential to meaningful pastoral care. A balance of traditional prayers and free praying is vital to vigorous and faithful prayerfulness. On the one hand, traditional prayers, such as the Lord's Prayer or prayers designated in various liturgies, provide a sense of order in pastoral ministry. They articulate and represent the continuity of all pastoral care with the worship of God's people, past and present. On the other hand, free prayers give wings to the content of traditional prayers. Free prayers are spontaneous, immediate, and particular.

To say prayers in public worship or in a pastoral care situation is not the same as praying. Praying is of the Spirit. Praying takes people out of themselves. Experientially, to pray is to enter transitional space, a place where subject-object relations are transcended. In transitional experiences such as praying, one discovers a different relationship between the established, inner representations of self and others, including God. When praying, one is engaged with what is beyond one's past knowing and believing. This is encounter with transcendent reality. Praying may begin with one's past images of God and one's belief concepts, but it is fresh with wonder and awe. When praying, people can make use of a familiar image in order to project themselves into transitional or sacred space, but once one is in that space praying becomes a fresh encounter with the transcendence of God. This experience calls for subsequent reflection that revises one's understanding of God and of oneself. To say that prayer is the soul of pastoral care is a way of pointing to the manner in which praying opens people to the ever-transcending reality of God.

This preliminary reflection on praying and transcendence discloses that the locus of God's reality is not reducible to what is simply inside or outside the praying person. Reflection affirms that God is deeper within than consciousness can discern and at the same time farther beyond any boundaries that human imaginations can fathom. The experienced absence of God is a way of remembering and longing for God as one has known God in the past. Just as significantly, the experienced absence of God is a way of waiting for God to be disclosed afresh. The elusive fascination with God rescues the praying person from enemies of the soul such as mere self-talk and mere knowledge.

Praying is like other forms of interpersonal knowing. Often people know far more than they realize, and so have to be reminded of what they already know. Yet just as often they discover that they do not know nearly what they assumed they knew about themselves and others. So it is that because persons have known God in some fashion in the past they now are are called to know God afresh—they are called to pray. And because they have believed in God already they now struggle with believing, with receiving the grace of God anew. Praying shows people the riches in their poverty. Because praying opens persons to the ever-transcending God, pastoral care is not so much ministering to others as it is being bom again with others. Such happenings are by God's grace, and praying is a means for receiving this grace.

An ordered pastoral care takes its clues from the prayers of the community of faith. A free pastoral care follows the lead of the spirit of these prayers as much as it repeats these prayers. A renewed pastoral care moves from prayer to praying, rediscovering the transcendent in the midst of human joy and suffering.

Scripture as the Substance

As the substance of pastoral care, Scripture is the source of true and truthful caring. Consequently, *lectio divina* (divine reading) is an essential dimension of pastoral care ministry. Traditionally, *lectio divina* has this structure: reading of the divine text, reflecting on the text, praying for the word to touch the heart, and contemplating and encountering the text in a silence too deep for words or thought. Whether or not this structure is followed precisely in a particular method of attending to Scripture, it identifies vital dimensions of listening to the word of God being spoken in people's lives today.

What does it mean to relate Scripture to pastoral care in a manner that balances freedom, order, and transcendence? Freedom entails praying the Scriptures and listening to God by studying the Scriptures. To be free in this praying means to have the capacity to go beyond wooden repetition of the words of Scripture. It points to the opportunity to discover the Spirit alive in the words. The Holy Spirit gives life to these ancient words so that they become holy words, aflame in the human heart here and now. To be free, then, means to hear the word of God speaking through Scriptures to us as we are situated in our present condition. The word of God liberates as the word discloses its new meaning. When pastors are ministering to others, they are listening with others for God's word. A fresh understanding is discovered, one that resonates with the spirit and original intent of the ancient words, yet represents a genuinely new level of apprehension and understanding.

Such freedom to listen to God's word with an open, inquiring spirit is strengthened by particular disciplines for attending to God's word: that is, disciplines of praying and exegeting the Scriptures. In this sense sustained freedom in attending to the word being spoken depends in part on the order derived from personal and community disciplines. Exegetical disciplines help persons to separate genuine freedom in understanding from fantasy and personal bias in their listening. Subsequently, their listening develops a discerning, critical edge. The hearing of God's word in public worship and the mutual correction that comes from classes and small-group Bible study provide structures that order the search for God's truth. The biblical canon as the basic rule of faith establishes the order of limits—Christians are not obligated to any and all rules for living, but to the Way presented concretely in the Christian canon. Such a canon is the seedbed in which the people of God nurture their growing identity and self-definition as a community of faith and as individual persons.

When the freedom of first impressions and spontaneous listening to God in daily life is balanced by exegetical and community disciplines, by careful and reverent attention to the Christian canon, a second naivete emerges as the shape of Christians' developing faith. This process involves an encounter with the transcendent dimension. Personal and community identities are challenged and transformed, and aspects of this process are ineffable. The Christian tradition thus reminds Christians of contemplation as silence, as being and attending beyond thought, although such contemplation is experienced as a standing on thought (the canon) and being lifted beyond those words and any of one's own.

These dimensions of the substance of pastoral care take shape in two major ways. One way is in liturgy as part of pastoral ministry, for Scripture permeates the liturgy. The liturgy is a way of presenting Scripture, both to the community of faith and to individuals and families in daily life. Liturgy, however, not only presents the words of Scripture—it also represents the spirit of the faith in form and symbol so that the word of God is presented to the whole community and to the whole person. The word is communicated verbally, dynamically with the energy of interpersonal action, and symbolically with objects that open the unconscious as well as the conscious mind to the presence of one who speaks of love, mercy, and justice. In presenting Scripture in pastoral care and counseling, one should not quote proof texts at people, but rather should position oneself to listen with them to the transcent word of God, which ordinarily takes the form of ritual action.

The second way in which the Scripture is presented in pastoral care is through the persons involved in any pastoral event. To some degree personal lives have been shaped and molded by God's word, and so the word is embodied, however imperfectly, in persons. Pastors pledge themselves to attend to the word of God in Scripture with the hope and trust that such disciplines will be means by which God becomes embodied in their lives and opens them to the presence of God in others. Just as prayerfulness is the soul of pastoral care, so truthfulness is the content of pastoral care, a truthfulness nurtured by Scripture. The truth of Scripture is made known by learning the interpretations of the past and by struggling with knowing anew. Christians are truthful when they stand by the profound understandings of their heritage, and they are truthful when they come to terms with their utter ignorance of God and God's truth, waiting until God presents truth to them as if for the first time. This truth is encapsuled in Scripture and represented subtly yet concretely in those destined to be God's living images—people.

Reconciliation as the Evangelical Principle

The evangelical principle of pastoral care is embodied in the ritual of reconciliation, a ritual that can have different names in various church traditions. Although embodied ritually in confession/absolution, this principle, qua principle, is normative for all pastoral care. Thus all pastoral care is meant to be evangelical in spirit, power, and significance.

An understanding of the evangelical principle as it takes ritual form should enable us to discern the elements of freedom, order, and transcendence in pastoral care.

A rite of reconciliation or confession/absolution is a vehicle for persons to bring everything to God in freedom, both particular wrongs and a core sense of being faulted as a community and as individuals. The rite is an invitation to be real before God, to cast aside pretense before others and the pride of self that precludes true self-knowing. It is the beginning of knowing self as one is known and the end of secure self-knowledge within the framework of what is fashionable and acceptable to one's self. To confess sinfulness in the light of God's truth and love is to become aware of being attended to by God. Evangelical faith made operational in confession is the basis for a new self-knowing, a self-understanding that liberates communities and persons from the self-serving and self-justifying demands of natural self-knowledge.

The freedom so prominent in such a rite is an ordered freedom. It takes the form of a ritual act, and such an act has a prelude and a sequel—it is a process as well as an event. The prelude may involve diverse experiences such as the collapse of a comfortable and stable self-image, or the kind of personal insights that emerge from personal psychotherapy, or a conflict in the community of faith that heightens awareness of the need for reconciliation. The sequel involves intentional and symbolic behaviors that give concrete expression to gratitude for forgiveness and to the faith that lays claim to God's promised transformation. New actions of the reconciled are not so much prescriptions for healing as they are an ongoing listening or attending to the absolution. In a sense these actions rehearse and recall the declaration of pardon; they celebrate God's liberating good news of mercy; they assert and proclaim that the grace of God creates true amendment of life; and they are particular behaviors that help the reconciled envision all the ways in which God's transforming grace is at work in their midst.

Because of the power of God's Spirit reconciling Christians through the priesthood of believers, they can declare forgiveness one to another.

To do that they employ symbolic acts—which in the past have been called "satisfaction"—that constitute a form of fulfillment of reconciliation. These acts are not satisfaction in the sense of being a condition or requirement for the completion of a promise, but they are the proper and dynamic sequels that help to give form to the satisfactory completion of Christ's ministry of reconciliation. This means that a vital link exists between the ministries of reconciliation and guidance. Those engaged in care may need to be more cautious than they have been about the degree to which they separate these ministries.

The transcendent dimension of the rite of reconciliation is most evident in the absolution. Here is God's word from beyond, a word to the community and to the person that makes its own claim and is not to be denied. Divine grace makes available one believer to another, so that the word of the transcendent God (visually absent) is encountered face to face. The sociality of this rite—its social structure—makes possible an immanent encounter with the transcendent.

The absolution, however, is not the only act in which transcendent power is operative. Genuine and substantive confession is not possible without a remembering, longing for, or affirmation of the prior reality of the God of justice and mercy. Confession itself is at least in part a coming to understand oneself in light of the Other. The subsequent actions undertaken in light of the divine forgiveness are symbolic, pointing beyond themselves and beyond the subjects who perform them to their true author, to God. The rite of reconciliation is a means of grace; as such it is neither a way of manipulating the self nor a form of self-help or self-progress. The self-esteem to which this rite gives birth is not founded on a self-understanding that exists prior to being known, forgiven, and enjoyed by God. The new self-regard is an expression of restored relationships, divine and human.

In the rite of reconciliation and in all evangelical expressions of pastoral care the presentation of God confronts persons with new self-images in relation to God and others. Ritual and communal and personal embodiments of the evangel enable new beginnings—a rebirth of love for God and others that feels wholly fresh and new. The evangelical principle gives pastoral care its marvelous and awesome energy, and the rite of reconciliation is its key ritual expression.

Baptism as the Liturgical Foundation

The evangelical principle of pastoral care is the exclusive focus of the rite of reconciliation. The principle is present in all pastoral ritual and ministry that is true to the gospel. It is no surprise, then, that the evangel is salient in baptism. Furthermore, as part of Christian initiation, baptism provides a ritual foundation for all pastoral care. With the new Roman Catholic rites for Christian initiation of adults as a basis for analysis and reflection, I have interpreted Christian rites of initiation, including baptism, as a model of God's transformation of human life, communal and individual. The Roman Catholic new rites contain communal, liturgical, pastoral, and personal elements. These diverse dimensions provide structure for the spiritual, social, and ethical qualities of the church's ministry of baptism. The sacrament of baptism in these rites is set within an ordered structure of preparation, initiation, and consolidation: the catechesis, the rites of initiation, and the *mystagogia*. The communal and personal aspects of faith are evident in this model when analyzed theologically and psychologically.

As the liturgical foundation and primary ritual source of pastoral care, baptism informs all pastoral care events. Premarital ministry was discussed as an example of how baptism serves in this foundational manner. In the course of that discussion it became clear that most forms of premarital ministry lack an explicitly ritual dimension; that criticism yielded a suggestion for a new ritual at the time of public engagement of a couple.

The ministry of baptism calls for a balance of freedom, order, and transcendence in all forms of pastoral care. The first freedom proclaimed in baptism is freedom from sin. Baptism does not literally and magically perfect communities or persons, but it declares and enacts the victory of divine grace over all aspects of human faultedness and brokenness. It provides a way to renounce evil, sin, and the devil and a way to affirm allegiance to the God of Jesus Christ. As the center of Christian initiation, baptism is the first example of these freedoms and so challenges all ritual and ministry to proclaim the universal liberation from sin and for God that is inaugurated in baptism. Grace means freedom, and baptism is the first ritual means whereby God's grace is freely given.

Given the spirit of freedom embodied in baptism, it is no surprise that this foundation makes room for ritual innovation in pastoral ministry. Most of today's Christian rituals were at one time innovations subsequent to the formative period of Christianity. The rites of reconciliation and of Christian marriage are examples. As it shapes present-day ministry, the freedom given in baptism enables those involved in pastoral care to be responsive to new conditions and needs by being innovative in every way, including new rituals. This freedom does not mean that anything goes, for every form of pastoral ministry, if it is to have integrity, must be built on the foundation of Christian baptism. Its origin and emergence from this foundation should be clear and compelling.

The sacrament or ordinance of baptism takes place within an ordered structure that involves (1) a period of preparation, (2) the event itself, and

(3) the ensuing consolidation of all that God has begun in this means of grace. Because of this one can envision an order in divine transformation of human life. This structure for channeling transformation has ritual, communal, pastoral, and personal elements. All of these are vital; none by itself is complete or a panacea. For example, it would be a mistake and an oversimplification to think that more ritual means better pastoral care. What goes before and comes after ritual is essential to the order of transformation. Liturgical transformation, transformation occurring in the transitional space of ritual experience, is destined to become transformation in all aspects of living. It is an enactment that calls Christians to the work of justice, to moral commitment, and to radically new behavior.

With baptism as its paradigm, transformation calls for new order. Transformation creates new structures in personal, community, political, and cultural life. When sensitive to its foundation in baptism, pastoral ministry is aware of this dynamic. Premarital ministry, for example, should be aware that preparation for marriage entails commitment to a new order. Two persons with previous commitments to family systems are preparing to become loyal to a new order and system. In this kind of change that calls for new order, all the persons and family systems involved undergo transformation. One task of pastoral care in such a situation is to assist and facilitate this transformation process so that it is free and stable. Such ministry can hope to be faithful when communal, educative, dynamic, and symbolic dimensions are integral to the process and integrated in it.

When these dimensions characterize pastoral ministry, the transcendent aspect of this ministry is more readily evident. Ritual actions prepare Christians to discern the symbolic in all actions. The death and rebirth enacted in baptism and realized by faith are transcendent realities in which persons participate. To disengage, to put to death the old self and all its relationships, is not a deed one undertakes oneself. To be engaged in a new life and all its relationships is to receive grace, to live by faith alone, to discover how it is that giving is an expression of having received. This is knowing the unknowable, experiencing the presence of mystery, and experiencing the reality of God in our midst yet not by our design or in our own image. Baptism and consequently all pastoral ministry celebrate and recognize the action of divine grace. Baptism is the deep, living spring from which pastoral ministry flows.

Eucharist as the Eschatological Horizon

Pastoral care has a horizon that predetermines or shapes its vision and that both orders it and set it free. Pastoral care's horizon is eschatological—its end is imminent.

This quality of Christian living and pastoral ministry is embodied most profoundly in the Eucharist, where Christians' host is the one who has come and who is coming again. Christ is present in a particular way, in the Spirit, through this event and its symbols of bread and wine. This is a sacramental presence, a presence in the midst of absence, a presence through presents or symbolic gifts. It is the presence of one who is about to come. In Christ the present is an actualized part of the whole, the promised future. By faith the promised future is prereceived in the present. God's presence in this event is a transitional presence, located between the past and the future in such a manner that the past is relived and the future foreknown in the present moment. The Eucharist opens up a sacred space where God is beyond knowing except in external symbols that transform the inner imagination.

The Eucharist is a thank offering. Through Christians' stewardship of the elements of nature, the objects become symbols of their thanks and their offering of themselves. In the same event the objects become symbols of God's self-offering, including passion and sacrifice, on human beings' behalf. The multiple meaningfulness of the elements, the manner in which they convey meaning both ways at once, displays the wondrous manner in which the divine and the human inhere and help to define each other. The Eucharist is a memorial that makes alive in the present the past passion and sacrifice of Jesus Christ and that makes present the communion of saints. It is a blessing that re-creates community and solidarity among Christians as they look to the promised future, the future God already has established and is about to bring to fruition. The Eucharist is an offering of Christians' transformed community and selves to the service of the future promises that already have converted them. The Eucharist is the gathering that sends Christians out. It is their commissioning.

By virtue of this means of grace Christians discover the freedom of being determined by their end. This is different from being determined by their past. Although each human being's origins are in God, each has placed herself or himself in captivity by yielding to a faulted inheritance from humankind's past behavior and from his or her own actions. There is an indescribable freedom in the grace of a capacity to anticipate God's promised future as one's end despite the position one has assumed. In a sense God's future repositions the people of God without their moving or repositioning themselves, thus delivering them from their own bondage. The freedom of the Eucharist is the freedom of hope, a grace that truly liberates.

As a consequence of this grace, the people of God are able to offer themselves and their gifts in the Eucharist. This ritual offering enacts the freedom of offering their daily lives to God, the God of the future. Because God is God Christians make this offering of themselves without strings attached—without controlling the future for themselves. By God's grace their offering becomes a pure act of trust and liberates them from the dominance of compulsive control. By this grace they learn not to be anxious about tomorrow. By this grace hand they hand the agenda back over to God.

The Eucharist is a celebration in faith by the community. Hence, the Eucharist celebrates and restores the order of being a community of faith. In the Eucharist Christians reenact their community by blessing one another, by passing the peace of God one to another, by discerning the presence of Christ in one another. Further, the visible community extends itself by distributing the Eucharist beyond the gathered ones to include the marginalized ones. In the Eucharist the visible community becomes one with the invisible community, the true community of saints. In the Eucharist Christians recognize the true head and host of their community, the Christ who orders the community and the love of all its members. Through this sacrament Christians rehearse and repeat a profound and pervasive pattern of genuine living, a pattern of receiving and giving. Because of this ordinance, the vision of life as offering reorders Christians' priorities and reorganizes their thinking. In light of the Eucharist, pastoral ministry seeks to discover the self-offering in all forms of ministry.

In the Eucharist time is transcended through its own structures. In the midst of a present absence a past presence lives again. A promised presence preshapes the present moment, causing the present to transcend itself. The absent one is present through faith as memory and anticipation. The Eucharist sets the stage on which God challenges the human habit of seeing the future only vaguely and as far removed. In this sacrament human beings are invited to imagine the future as it may appear to God—as just now about to happen. This challenge corrects ordinary perceptions in a radical way. It cuts across calculations and redirects imagination. It undermines prediction and projects present human brokenness into an entirely other and yet near-to-hand future—it prophesies. The Eucharist transcends ordinary ways of being together and of self-understanding, and so it transforms. In response to the promises of God in the Eucharist, Christians offer themselves to the Transcendent One and so discover the way of self-transcendence.

Because of the Eucharist, pastoral care is both priestly and prophetic. In pastoral ministry one witnesses to an undefined yet undeniable presence wherever absence is found. Whether being present where there is agony and alienation or challenging lethargy and halfhearted living, ministry that is eucharistic in its basic self-understanding serves the present situation because it belongs to the future. It breathes the divine life of the future into the struggling present.

The Means of Grace as Pastoral Care

As pastoral care ministry comes to give more attention to the means of grace—exemplified in this book by prayer, *lectio divina* (divine reading), the rite of reconciliation, baptism, and the Eucharist—it will be renewed with a richer and more vigorous admixture of freedom, order, and transcendence. The theological and psychological analyses proffered in this book disclose the vital significance of such means of grace for ministry that is to be truly pastoral and genuinely caring. My analysis has emphasized the image of ordained ministers as representatives. Ordained ministers are entrusted to take initiative in the use of ritual and symbolic acts, and to administer sacraments and ordinances. Certain lay orders and lay positions also embody a representative and pastoral role. All these persons, clergy and lay, re-present Christian faith and tradition in their being, in their caring, and in appropriate means of grace. Their ministry presents God anew so that both others and they themselves are caught up in awe, love, and faith. And they re-present persons to themselves, assisting them to envision God's unique work and presence in their lives.

This examination and reflection still leaves room for differing understandings of the ordinances and sacraments and of the particular forms ministers follow in various traditions of the Christian faith. Let us hope that the current renewal of interest, to which this book endeavors to contribute, stimulates vigorous as well as productive dialogue and debate for the enrichment of pastoral ministries.

Index

Absence, 134
  See also God, Absence of
Absolution
  definition of, 70
  as proclamation, 74
Acceptance
  of persons, 67
  of self and others, 132
American Association of
  Pastoral Counselors, 3
Anglican tradition, 75
Anointing, 99, 100
Apostles' Creed, 93–94, 100
Ashbrook, J. B., n.106
Association of Clinical
  Pastoral Education, 3
Attentiveness, 42, 61
  to Scripture, 64
Augustine, St., 62
Authority, 58
Autonomy, 69
Availability, 131–32

Baptism, 150–52
  adult rite, 97–101
  of infants and children,
    108–10
  renewal of, 110–13
  *Baptism, Eucharist, and
    Ministry*, 85
Baptist tradition, 86
Barnhouse, R. Tiffany, n.38
Barth, K., 19
Berrigan, D., 21

Bible
Exodus
  chapter 3: 16
  chapter 12: 52
Ezra
  chapter 3: 138
Psalms, 26, 42–43, 45
  Psalm 27: 26
  Psalm 52: 37
  Psalm 88: 26
  Psalm 121: 138
  Psalm 126: 138
Malachi
  chapter 3: 130
Matthew, 127
  chapter 9: 54
Luke
  chapter 1: 49, 50, 54
  chapter 9: 54
  chapter 24: 54-55
John, 92, 127
  chapter 3: 119, 107
  chapter 6: 56
  chapter 10: 51, 101
  chapter 14: 51
  chapter 16: 55
Acts
  chapter 17: 54
Romans
  chapter 6: 100, 107
  chapter 12: 121
1 Corinthians
  chapter 3: 32

  chapter 6: 107
  chapter 10: 107
2 Corinthians
  chapter 5: 55, 77
Galatians
  chapter 3: 107
Ephesians
  chapter 4: 53
  chapter 5: 107
Colossians
  chapter 1: 54
  chapter 2: 107
2 Timothy
  chapter 3: 49
Titus
  chapter 3: 107
Hebrews
  chapter 2: 64
1 Peter
  chapter 3: 107
2 Peter
  chapter 1: 57
Revelation
  chapter 3: 138.
Blessing, 125–26, 132–33
  of the water, 98–99
Boisen, A. T., 3, 9, 56, 58,
  138
Bonhoeffer, D., 42, 74
Brooke, R., 56
Bruner, J., 24
Burke, K., 80
Burnish, R., n.94, 104

157

160 Pastoral Care and the Means of Grace

Privatization, 112–13
Psychoanalysis, 30
Pruyser, P. W., 51, 132
Psychotherapy, 58–59, 62,
  69, 78–79, 84
Purification, 90–95
Purity, 54

Ramshaw, E., 132
Rational-emotive
  psychotherapy, 108
Rauschenbusch, W., 3
Reconciliation, 149–50
  psychological analysis of,
    76–79
  and psychotherapy, 84
  theological
    understandings, 68–76
Redemption, 80
Reformation, 7, 69
Reformed tradition, 4, 74–
  75
Regression, 30, 43
Religious
  definition, 2
  language, 6
  resources, 1, 2
  See also Means of grace
Renewal
  See Baptism, renewal of
  liturgical, 3–4
  religious, 4–5
  spiritual, 8
Rites of Initiation, 97–104
Rizzuto, Ana-Maria, 26, 79,
  107
Role, Pastor's, 57–59
Roman Catholic Church, 4,
  70–71, 85–87, 130
Rufus, M., 43

Sacred space, 14–19
  psychology of, 23–30
  theology of, 14–23
Sacrifice, 126–28
Sanctuary, 17

Schmemann, A., 97
Scripture and pastoral
  conversations, 59
Scrutinies, 91–93
Self-acceptance, 28
Self
  false, 54, 62
  image, 35, 56, 77–78
  new, 60, 83
  and other relationships,
    origin of, 23–25
  sociality of, 39
  talk, 47, 60
  trust, 51, 53
  See also Images; Prayer as
    self–talk
Service, 128
Shaw, G. B., 75
Shepherding image, 15, 16
Shut-in persons, 134
Sick and Dying, renewal of
  baptism for, 112
Sin, *See* Confession of Sin;
  Faultedness
Smith, M. L., n.69
Smith, J. Z., 2
Socrates, 53
Soul, 31
Spirituality, 4
Spiritual direction, 40
Steiner, G., 5
Stone, H., 55, 59
Subject and object, 129, 146
  as object, 37
Symbol, 31–32, 39, 43, 47,
  62, 76, 118

Taizé community, 123, 126
Terrien, S. L., 22
Texts
  classic, 10, 11, 64
  pastoral, 9, 11–12
  primordial, 64
Thank offering, 119–123,
  153
Theory, 9

Thurian, M., n.123,
  n.126,127, n.128, n.132
Tidball, D. 11–12
Tillich, P., 5
Timaeus, 53
Transcendence 1–2, 7, 59,
  61, 95–96
  and baptism, 152
  and the Eucharist, 154
  and *lectio divina*, 148
  and prayer, 146
  and reconciliation, 150
Transference, 43, 63, 84
Transformation 7, 20, 82–
  83, 130, 143
  and baptism, 103, 106,
    108, 113
Transitional object, 32, 39,
  43, 106
  special, 28
Transitional reality, 54
Transitional space, 24–25,
  44, 60–61, 86, 129
Truth, 44, 56, 148
Turner, V., 16, n.17, 32

Ulanov, A., n.35
Ulanov, B., n.35
Underwood, R. L., n.133

Vatican II, 57, 70, 87, 108,
  112
Vocation, 112, 122

Wainwright, G., n.123,
  n.126, n.128
Watts, F., n.8, n.31
Weil, L., 20–21, 31
Weil, S., 26, 31
Wesley, J., 7, 75–76
Williams, D. D., 81
Williams, M. G., n.8, n.31,
  n.106
Winicott, D. W., 31
Word of God, 72, 96
  psychological aspects, 53–
    55
  theology of, 72, 76